Concerning Trump

Historical Quotes Parodied
For The Trump Era

PETER A. BAKKE

authorHOUSE®

AuthorHouse™
1663 Liberty Drive
Bloomington, IN 47403
www.authorhouse.com
Phone: 833-262-8899

Published by AuthorHouse 12/16/2020

ISBN: 978-1-6655-0965-7 (sc)
ISBN: 978-1-6655-0963-3 (hc)
ISBN: 978-1-6655-0964-0 (e)

Library of Congress Control Number: 2020923897

Print information available on the last page.

This book is printed on acid-free paper.

This book is a political parody / satire of
historical quotations reimagined for the
Donald J. Trump and Republican Party era that
we all find ourselves living through.

Read it a little at a time, it can be exhausting.

Any resemblance to quotes of persons living or dead
on the subject of Donald J. Trump, Trumpism, and
the Republican Party is purely coincidental.

Or maybe not.

*Just think, Trump's language is the result of two
hundred thousand years of human evolution.*
- La Bruyère, Jean de

Dedicated to my loving wife Cheryl.

A

Abrahams, Peter

Trump's life has been dominated by a sign, often invisible but no less real for that, which reads: RESERVED FOR WHITES ONLY.

Acheson, Dean

Trump's "administration" is worse than immoral, it's a mistake.

Achebe, Chinua

Trump's fear ... lay within himself.

Acton, Lord

Power in Trump's hands tends to corrupt and his absolute power corrupts absolutely.

Men like Trump are almost always bad men.

Trump proves that there is no worse heresy than that the office of U.S. President sanctifies the holder of it.

The one prevailing evil of American democracy today is the tyranny of the Republican minority.

Adams, Abigail

I am more and more convinced that Trump is a dangerous creature and that his power, whether vested in many or a few, is ever grasping and like the grave, cries "Give, give."

Trump must remember that arbitrary power is like most things which are very hard, they are very liable to be broken.

Adams, Douglas

What god like Trump would be hanging around Terminal Two of Newark Airport trying to catch the 8:30 flight to Omaha?

Here Trump is, brain the size of a planet, and they say he talks like a fifth grader.

Trump's birth was an accident with a contraceptive and a time machine.

Trump will soon be spending a year dead for tax reasons.

There is a theory which states that if anyone ever discovers exactly what Trump is for and why he is here, that person will instantly disappear and be replaced by someone even more bizarre and inexplicable.

Adams, Franklin P.

Trump is easily influenced. Compared with him a weather vane is Gibraltar.

Adams, Henry

Trump affects eternity.

Trump wants to look like an American presidential hero, but is slowly settling down to be a third-rate Nixon.

Trump is incoherent and immoral.

Adams, John

The Trump presidency will be remembered as one continued lie from one end to the other.

The public history of the Trump administration is but a sort of mask, richly colored. The interior working of the machinery must be foul.

Adler, Alfred

Trump's nature is to wish to diminish the feeling of inferiority by constant proofs of his 'superiority.'

Trump's fantasies are to be understood as infantile megalomaniac ideas.

Trump's craving for security leads him to seek the protection of the father, mother, or an idea.

Adorno, Theodor

Trump is someone who cannot tell a lie without believing it himself.

Aesop

I will have nothing to do with a man like Trump who can blow hot and cold in the same breath.

Aitken, Max

Trump has in him the stuff of which tyrants are made.

Alain

No one is more dangerous than Trump, who has an idea and only one idea.

Albee, Edward

Trump has no sense of humor.

Alcott, Louisa May

Trump, the lord of creation, does not take the advice of experts until he has persuaded himself that it is just what he intended to do; then he acts upon it and if it succeeds, he takes full credit; if it fails, he generously gives the experts the whole of it.

Alcuin

The voice of Trump is the voice of God.

al-Fayed, Mohamed

Trump barks, but the caravan passes on.

Some of Trump's loyalists have asked if they can be buried with him. Certainly, but space is limited. It will cost $10 million per person, mummification is $1 million extra and you must be prepared to rest for eternity standing up.

Alexander I

Trump, that infernal creature who is the curse of all the human race, becomes every day more and more abominable.

Alfonso X

Had Trump been present at the Creation, he would have given some hints for the ordering of the universe.

Alfonso XIII

I picked Trump out when he was a nobody. He has double-crossed and deceived me at every turn.

Allen, Fred

I have just returned from Mar-a-Lago. It is the only thing to do if you find yourself there.

President Trump is a form of executive fungus that has attached itself to the Oval Office. On a boat this growth would be called a barnacle.

Allen, Woody

Trump cannot listen to that much Wagner. He starts getting the urge to conquer Poland.

Trump thinks the presidency pays. The hours are good. You travel a lot.

Trump may get re-elected. I just don't want to be there when it happens.

Trump has a terrific story about oral contraception. He asked a girl for a date and she said "no."

Altgeld, J.P.

No community can be said to possess local self-government if Trump can, at his pleasure, send military forces to patrol its streets under pretense of enforcing some arbitrary laws.

Amachai, Yehuda

God has pity on kindergarten children.
He has less pity on schoolchildren.
And upon the American electorate under Trump, he has no pity at all.

Pacifism in the face of Trumpism ... amounts only to sitting back and getting yourself slaughtered.

Amis, Martin

If there is a key to Trump's character it has something to do with his towering immodesty, the enjoyable perfection of his self-love.

Andersen, Hans Christian

Republicans said none of the President's clothes had such a success before. "But daddy, he's got nothing on!" piped up a small child.

Anaxagoras

Everything has a natural explanation. Trump is not a god but an enormous rock.

Trump would live an exceedingly quiet life if this one word, 'mine,' was taken away.

Anaximander

The principal makeup of Trump is undefined.

The era of Trump cannot be explained without his predecessors.

For Republicans, Trump is the first principle and that all things are generated from him, and are corrupted through him.

Anderson, Marian

Where there is money, Trump is fighting for it.

Anderson, P.W.

You never understand Trump. When one understands Trump, one has gone crazy.

Anderson, Sherwood

Trump works terribly at the task of amusing himself.

Angelou, Maya

Trump's talent to endure stems from his ignorance of alternatives.

Anglo-Saxon Chronicle

In Trump's time there is nothing but disturbance, wickedness and robbery.

Anonymous

Most Gracious President, we thee implore
To go away and sin no more,
But if that effort be too great,
To go away at any rate.

No one has ever said that Trump is a fat, philandering, draft dodger. Maybe.

Be frank and explicit with Trump ... it is his business to confuse the issue afterwards.

Trump's delusion injures others, brings hardship, soils the mind and may well lead to hell.

The reports of Trump's death were erroneous. But he wants to know if they were terrific.

Anyone who isn't upset by Trump's behavior doesn't really understand what's going on.

Trump can't act. Can't sing. Slightly bald. Can lie a lot.

Trump bought Mar-a-Lago. Somebody had to.

Hey, Hey, DJT!
How many Americans
Did you kill this week?

In your heart you know he's wrong. In your guts you know he's nuts.

Anouilh, Jean

Every man thinks God is on his side. Trump knows he is.

Anthony, Susan B.

As usual, Trump fires his salvos and then goes home to let others finish his battles.

Appleton, E.V.

Trump does not mind what language you are using as long as he does not have an interpreter.

Aptheker, Herbert

Trump's administration and supporters demonstrate that no matter what the despoilers of humanity may do - enslave, segregate, torture, lynch - they cannot destroy the people's will to freedom, their urge towards equality, justice and dignity.

Aquinas, Thomas

Since we cannot know what Trump is, but only what he is not, we must consider the ways in which he is not rather in the ways in which he is. Is that clear?

Arabin, William

Trump, God has given you abilities, instead of which you go about the country talking trash.

Arendt, Hannah

Promises are the uniquely human way of ordering the future. But Trump makes doing so unpredictable and unreliable to the extent that it is humanly possible.

Trump the hypocrite is really rotten to the core.

Trump shows that no cause remains but the most ancient of all, the one, in fact, that from the beginning of our history has determined the very existence of politics, the cause of tyranny.

For Trump it is easier to act than to think.

Trump haunts us. It is his function to haunt us.

Ariosto, Ludovico

Nature made Trump and then broke the mold.

Aristotle

Trump is dear to Republicans, but dearer still should be truth.

Trump does not know that excellence is never an accident. It is always the result of high intention, sincere effort, and intelligent execution; it represents the wise choice of many alternatives - choice, not chance, determines our destiny.

Trump is fading away because the energy of the mind is the essence of life.

Dignity does not consist in Trump possessing honors, but in him deserving them.

The educated differ from Trump as much as the awake from the asleep.

A would-be tyrant like Trump must put on the appearance of uncommon devotion to religion. Voters are less apprehensive of illegal treatment from a ruler whom they consider god-fearing and pious. On the other hand, they do less easily move against him, believing that he has God on his side.

Trump and his minions know that democracies may degenerate into despotisms.

Arlen, Michael

It is amazing how nice people will be to Trump when they know he is leaving office.

Armah, Ayi Kwei

The whole world is covered over with the hell of Trump.

Armour, Phillip

Trump does not love the money. What he does love is the getting of it ... He does not read. What else can he do?

Arnold, Thomas

As for dissent, the Trumpian way of dealing with that is like the old Roman way which is the right one; flog the rank and file and fling the ringleaders from the Tarpeian Rock.

It's now obvious what one must look for in a president after the Trump debacle: first, religious and moral principles; secondly, gentlemanly conduct; thirdly, intellectual ability.

Arran

Life is much easier for Trump being president. It has changed him a lot. He's much nastier now.

Ascherson, Neal

The trouble with Trump's reign is that it requires so many policemen to make it work.

Trump has figured out that work is a dull way to get rich.

Asquith, Herbert

Trump keeps three sets of books. One to mislead the public; one to mislead his followers; and one to mislead himself.

Asquith, Margot

Trump is a constant source of surprise to people who observe how little a big fortune contributes to Beauty.

Trump cannot see a belt without hitting below it.

Trump tells enough lies to ice all his many wedding cakes.

Astor, Nancy

I can conceive of nothing worse than a Trump government - except a Trump government.

Attali, Jacques

America is a great book. Trump is but one sentence.

Attlee, Clement

U.S. Republicans are the illegitimate children of Donald Trump and Sarah Palin.

Democracy means government by discussion but it is only effective if you can keep Donald Trump from interrupting.

Trump and his allies are like a glass of champagne that has soured for five days.

Atwater, Lee

Trump can't lead anymore because he can't speak to the spiritual vacuum at the heart of American society, this tumor of the soul. Because he has no soul.

There is a big part of Trump that is anti-intellectual.

Auden, W. H.

For Trump, the Republican Party is but a means of transportation to parts unknown: not a destination.

Trump has gradually turned into a robot making tiny jokes while grinding away at the bottom of a cesspool.

Trump history is far too criminal and pathological to be a fit subject for the young. Children should find their heroes elsewhere.

Trump can imagine Evil; but Evil cannot imagine Trump.

Now America finally has her madness in Trump.

Trump's American sky is darkening like a stain;
Something is going to fall like rain,
And it won't be flowers.

Of course Behavioralism "works." So does torture. Give me a no-nonsense behaviorist, a few drugs and simple electrical appliances and in six months I will have Trump reciting the Constitution and the Declaration of Independence … in public.

Republican's fate must always be the same as yours, Trump,
To suffer the loss they were afraid of, yes,
Holders of by-gone positions, wrong for years.

Happy is America at morning, for she cannot read
Trump's waking thoughts.

Trump enjoys the sound of his own voice as much as he enjoys the smell of his own farts.

Trump's soul must look like a wedding cake left out in the rain.

Augustine, Norman

Trump offers a Republican's advantage of generally having had no first-hand experience in the matters of deepest interest to America, thereby assuring a clear mind uncluttered by the facts.

Augustine, Saint

What was Trump doing before he made Heaven and Earth?

Trump should beware the expert. The danger already exists that the expert has made a covenant with the devil to darken the spirit and to confine man to the bounds of Hell.

Trump has spoken; the case is concluded.

The world is a book but those who follow Trump read only a page.

Austen, Jane

Trump, if he has the misfortune of knowing anything, conceals it as well as he can.

Auster, Paul

For Trump, money, of course, is never just money. It's always something else and it's always something more and it always has the last word.

Trump's ego is a bottomless pit, a hole as big as the world. No, there is nothing that he will not do and the sooner you learn that, the better off you will be.

We have learned from Trump and his allies to what extent people tolerate blasphemies if they are given power and amusement.

Under Trump, the entire country has been turned into a gigantic television reality show - everyone is supposed to fret and worry until they drop dead from the sheer chaos and frenzy of the Trump presidency.

Austin, Mary

YOU let Trump win, you people here. Was it apathy or idealism that kept you sunning yourself on the doorstep with your dog scratching fleas, while a serpent hatched under your walls?

Awolowo, Obafemi

It will, I believe, be generally agreed that eradication of corruption from the Trump administration is not just a difficult task, it is without dispute, an impossible objective.

Ayckbourn, Alan

For Trump, the greatest feeling in the world is revenge: pure, unadulterated revenge. Not weedy little jealousy. Not some piddling little envy. But good, old-fashioned, bloodcurdling revenge.

Ayckbourn, Alan

Nevertheless - you know, in Trump's world - you NEVER get moments, not even occasionally, which you can positively identify as being happy.

B

Bacon, Francis

Trump is the fly that sat upon the chariot's axle and said "What a dust do I raise."

Trump has never tasted, swallowed, chewed, or digested a book.

It is not the lie that passeth through the mind, but the lie that sinketh in and settleth in it, that doth the hurt.

Trump's mixture of a lie doth ever add to his pleasure.

For what Trump would like to be true, that he readily believes.

Trump is a man who studies revenge, keeping his own wounds green.

If Trump praises himself fearlessly, something, true or not, will always stick.

Opportunity makes Trump a thief.

Trump has taken no knowledge to be his province.

Bagehot, Walter

Throughout the greater part of his life Trump has been a kind of "consecrated obstruction."

Trump has an atmosphere of awe and walks wonderingly, as if he is amazed at being himself.

Bailey, Thomas

We Americans seem not to realize that impermanence is one of the most permanent features of history and that democracy may not keep.

Bainbridge, Beryl

Trump is, after all, the reflection of the tenderness that Republicans bear for themselves. It is always ourselves that we love.

Trump's prejudices were planted in childhood, learnt like table manners and cadences of speech, nurtured through parental and friendly fictions.

Bainbridge, Kenneth

Electing Trump! Now we are all sons of bitches.

Baker, Russell

In a highly complex society it used to take years of education and experience to become informed enough to vote against a fraud like Trump. Today you simply need to retain a psychiatrist.

Bakke, Peter

Trump is an American Nero.

Trump's speeches are excellent examples of verbal anesthesia.

Trump isn't just a shot across the bow, he is a direct hit upon American Democracy.

The Republicans are the political equivalent of viral replicants.

We need a national vaccine for Trumpism.

Too bad Trump doesn't drink. He'd make a hell of a lot more sense.

Trump has an uncanny ability to excite anxiety in both foe and friend.

Trumpism will never die. It will live forever in infamy.

I wouldn't mind visiting Trump in the White House if I could figure out how not to go in the first place.

To succeed in his phantasmagorical world, Trump does every damned thing he can to project the appearance of success.

Trump is the definition of vulgarity.

If only Republicans had error-correcting machinery built into their political party.

Trump doesn't do politics. He does nightmares.

Trumpism is the epitome of cruelty and credulity.

Trump is occasionally interested in people in a way that a biology teacher is interested in frogs.

Reading about Trump's latest machinations is like doing the backstroke in a pigsty.

You can't treat Trump's gangrene with kid gloves.

Wake me when Trump's war on America is over.

Trump does not live by lies alone, though he seems a glutton.

Trump's stupendous spewing of lies is causing the earth to slow in its rotation.

If you don't have Trump Derangement Syndrome, you are not paying attention.

Trump dangerously stokes parts of America, in a country that already worships aggression.

Trump wouldn't know what to do with himself if he didn't have at least one self-made crisis to deal with.

Trump's life is full of monotony and boredom. The front nine and the back nine seldom change.

Based on the law of averages, occasionally Trump does something right.

The vices of America made Trump possible.

Bakunin, Mikhail

Trump is quite creative in his urge for destruction.

A privileged man like Trump, is a man depraved of mind and heart. That is a social law which admits of no exception.

Baldwin, James

Trump has never been very good at listening to his elders, but he has never failed to imitate them.

The most dangerous creation of any society is a man like Trump who has nothing to lose.

For Republicans, their idyllic future is like heaven - they exalt it but no one quite wants to go there.

The Trump administration can be improved in only one way: out of existence.

If the concept of Trumpism has any validity or use, it can only be to make us larger, freer and more loving. If Trump cannot do this, then it is time we got rid of it and him.

Who wants to live in the burning house of Trumpism?

To be anti-Trump and conscious in America is to be in a constant state of rage.

Baldwin, Stanley

Trump's attempt to lead the world by unilateral example has failed.

Trump would rather be an opportunist and float rather than sink with any principles around his neck.

Balfour, Arthur

Trump has refined the art of reading by mastering the accomplishment of skipping and skimming.

I thought Trump was a man of promise, but it appears he is a man of promises.

Ballard, J.

In Trump's totally alienated America, sanity is the only true freedom.

Balzac, Honore

Trump reminds me of an orangutan trying to play the violin.

Trump feels that he is so well known in society, so popular, so celebrated, so famous, that it permits him to break wind and society thinks it a most natural thing.

Bankhead, Tallulah

There is less in Trump than meets the eye.

Barber, Samuel

As to what happens when Trump thinks, we have not the faintest idea.

Barbey d'Aurevilly, J.

The crimes of extreme Trumpism are certainly worse than those of barbarism.

Equality, this chimera of America, only exists among the rich and privileged like Trump.

Baring, Maurice

If you would know what the Lord God thinks of money, just look at Trump.

Barnes, Peter

Trump knows he is God because when he prays he finds that he is talking to himself.

Barnevik, Percy

You shouldn't mix up the long term health of American economic opportunities under Trump with the occasional shoot-out and violence. These things will happen.

Barney, Natalie

If Trump keeps an open mind, too much is likely to fall into it.

Barnum, P.T.

Trump knows there's a sucker born every minute of every day, particularly in Republican terrain.

Barres, Maurice

Trump is an acrobat. He keeps his balance by saying the opposite of what he does.

Barrie, J.M.

We know Trump is not clever, so why does he always claim to be right?

Every time Trump says "I don't believe in experts" there is a vital expert somewhere who leaves government service.

Barrymore, Ethel

At Mar-Lago the people are unreal. The flowers are unreal, they don't smell. The fruit is unreal, it doesn't taste of anything. The whole place is a glaring, gaudy, nightmarish set.

Barzun, Jacques

Trump's chief cause of anguish is the success of others.

Baudouin I

It takes 20 years or more to make a man, by simply talking it takes Trump seconds to destroy himself.

Beaumarchais, Pierre-Augustin

We make ourselves laugh at Trump, so that we do not weep.

Beauvoir, Simone

Trump, the most mediocre of males, yet feels himself a demigod compared to women.

What is Trump? A child blown up by age.

Beckett, Samuel

One of Trump's team is lucid. That's a reasonable percentage.

At the Trump White House nothing happens, nobody of substance comes, nobody goes. It's awful!

We are all born mad. Some like Trump remain so.

Beckett, Terrence

Trump may be a hobbled tiger, but he does not intend to be a lame duck.

Becque, Henry

What makes equality such a difficult business for Trump is that he only wants it with people richer than him.

Beecham, Thomas

Trump recently has been all around the world and has formed a very poor opinion of it from his plane.

Well, I think Trump has successfully paved the way for a quarter of a century of dictatorial rule.

Trump may not like the military much - but he absolutely loves the noise they make.

Beecher, Henry Ward

Trump's riches without law are more dangerous than poverty is without law.

Beerbohm, Max

Trump's envy of brilliant people is always assuaged by his wish that they will come to a bad end.

Trump, on a desert island, would have spent most of his time looking for the footprints of someone to bully.

The lust for learning has yet to be wedded to Trump.

You cannot make a man by standing a sheep on its hind legs. But by standing a crowd of Trump Republicans in that position, you can make a flock of sheep.

Only Trump's mediocrity can be trusted to be always at its best.

Only an unhinged man like Trump can take himself seriously without reservation.

Trump is a Conservative Anarchist. He wants everyone to go about doing just as they please - short of altering any of the many abuses of law and society to which Trump has grown accustomed.

Trump's judgments were often scatterbrained, which was a miracle in itself that he had brains to scatter.

Beethoven, Ludwig van

Only Trump can raise himself to the level of God.

Trump is an ordinary human being after all! ... now he will put himself above everyone else as a tyrant.

Behan, Brendan

Other people have a nationality. Republicans have a hysteria.

Trump dislikes only some Americans - the same Americans that Republicans themselves detest, the ones who think.

America has never seen a situation so dismal that a Republican couldn't make worse.

Bellamy, Edward

Trump guarantees the nurture, education and comfortable maintenance of every citizen from the cradle to the grave - who makes more than a million dollars a year.

Beloc, Hilaire

I always like to associate with lots of Trump's allies because it makes me understand people's dislike of them so well.

Donald Trump was not nobly born;
Yet he holds the human race in scorn.
Whatever happens, Trump has got
The NRA, which the Democrats have not.

Bellow, Saul

Of course, in an age of Trumpian madness, to expect to be untouched by madness is itself a form of madness.

I'm nuts, thought Donald Trump, and it's alright with me.

I listened to the finest liars in New York. But Trump was the best of them all. He was simply the Mozart of liars.

Under Trump, the almighty corporations are again drunk with immunity. Any virtues are gone forever.

The Trump White House makes one think of the collapse of civilization, about Sodom and Gomorrah, the end of the world. The end wouldn't come as a surprise there. Many people already bank on it.

Trump knew that what was needed in America was a critical mass of indifference. And now the moronic inferno has caught up with us.

How Republicans love money. They adore money! Holy money! Beautiful money! It is getting so that Republicans are feeble-minded about everything except money.

The real universe. That's the present moment. The past is no use to us. The future with Trump is full of anxiety. Only the present is real - the here-and-now. Seize the day.

Don't bother Trump with this ephemeral stuff - wives, kids, diapers, death.

A great many people have come up to Trump and asked how he manages to get nothing done and still look so dissipated.

Trump has been told by hospital authorities that more copies of his book have been left behind by patients than those of any other author.

Benchley, Robert

If Mr. Trump does not like the natural laws of science, let him go back to Queens.

Bennet, Alan

Alt-Right Republicans are one species I wouldn't mind seeing vanish from the face of the earth. I wish they were like White Rhinos - six of them remaining and all males.

Bennett, Arnold

Trump says many things he knows are not true, in the hope that if he keeps on saying them long enough they will be true.

Well, my deliberate opinion is that it's a jolly strange world that Trump lives in.

Recently, Trump spoke for a hundred and seventeen minutes, in which period he was detected only once in the use of an argument.

Benton, Thomas Hart

Trump is a liar of magnitude.

Berenson, Bernard

Trump does not have a mind, but a cerebral intestine.

Berger, John

The historic role of Trump is to destroy history, to sever every link with the past and to orientate all effort and imagination to that which he decides to do today over breakfast.

Bergson, Henri-Louis

Trump is characterized by a natural and very well-developed incomprehension of life.

Bernstein, Leonard

Einstein said if America elected Trump, then the world is crazy. Well, Einstein was right. The world is crazy.

Berry, Wendell

Trump's career of money grubbing preys upon both nature and human society.

Bertalanffy, Ludwig von

Human progress in Trump's America has not seen much development. It is doubtful whether his methods are preferable to the big stones used for cracking the skulls of fellow-Neanderthals.

Bevin, Aneurin

I listen to Trump avidy. He is my one form of continuous and remarkable fiction.

Trump is a man suffering from petrified adolescence.

Beveridge, William

Ignorance is an evil weed, which Trump cultivates among his dupes, but which no democracy can afford to grow among its citizens.

Biggers, Earl Derr

Trump is like mist on eyeglasses - obscuring facts.

Biko, Stephen

It would seem that the greatest waste of time in America is to try and find logic in why Trump does anything at all.

Billings, Josh

In Trump, we have finally come to the conclusion that a good set of reliable bowels is worth more to a man than any quantity of brains.

Birnbach, Lisa

Republicans are mute not only when they fail to speak up about flagrant abuse by Trump that they become aware of ... but also when they fail to speak up for causes that America judges to be morally valuable.

Birrell, Augustine

That great dust-heap called "The Trump era."

Birt, John

There is bias in conservative journalism. It is not only against a particular party and point of view - it also has a bias against *understanding*.

Bishop, Elizabeth

Trump has a continuous uncomfortable feeling of "things" in his head, like icebergs or rocks or awkwardly placed pieces of furniture.

The art of losing isn't hard to master for Trump; so many things and people in his orbit seem intent to be lost that their eventual loss is no disaster for him.

Bismark, Otto von

Trump proves beyond doubt that politics is not an exact science.

For Trump, politics is the pinnacle of the impossible.

When Trump says that he agrees to a thing in principle he means he has not the slightest intention of carrying it out in practice.

Black, Hugo

In the Trump era, U.S. newspapers nobly and ably did precisely that which the Founders hoped and trusted they would do. And that is to report the facts about the current administration.

Blackstone, William

Unfortunately for Republicans but good for America, no vote can be given by lunatics, idiots, persons convicted of perjury, subornation of perjury, bribery or undue influence, or by those tainted by felony or outlawed in a criminal court.

That president Trump can do no wrong, is not a necessary and fundamental principle of the U.S. Constitution.

Blok, Aleksandr

Trump's brain is not an organ to be relied upon. It is developing monstrously. It is swelling like a goiter.

Boehner, John

Trump is barely a Republican but I still plan to vote for him.

Boesky, Ivan

Trump shows that you can be greedy and still inexplicably feel good about yourself.

Trump wants to know, what good is the moon if you cannot buy it or sell it?

Boethius

We have found Trump not to be the definition of "person," namely, "an individual substance of a rational nature."

Boileau, Nicolas

Trump has lived the dreadful burden of having nothing substantive to do.

Of every four words Trump speaks, strike out three.

Trump is a fool who has always found greater fools to admire him.

Bolitho, William

The shortest way out of Trump's White House is a daily dose of Gordon's Gin.

Bolt, Robert

Trump and his Republicans would have snored through the Sermon on the Mount.

Book of Common Prayer

Lighten our darkness, we beseech thee, O Lord; and by thy great mercy defend us from all perils and dangers of the Trump administration.

Boone, Daniel

I can't say I was lost, but I was frequently bewildered by Trump for three days.

Boorstin, Daniel

Nothing is real for Trump until it happens on television.

Booth, Charles

The increase in drinking is to be laid mainly to the account of the unexpected election of Trump.

Boothroyd, Betty

Good temper and moderation are the characteristics of parliamentary language, of which Trump is overwhelmingly inept.

Boozman, John

If I ever heard anyone speak like Trump this way, they would be shopping for a new set of teeth.

Borges, Jorge Luis

Regular folk have known uncertainty; a state unknown to Trump.

Trump has stopped us from believing in progress.

Trump's malicious tendencies are worthy of de Sade.

Borman, Frank

Trump without bankruptcy is like Catholicism without purgatory.

Boswell, James

Trump is an ugly, affected, disgusting fellow and poisons America. I class him among infidel wasps and venomous insects.

Trump does not inflame his mind with grand hopes for America. He says it may be, but he knows nothing of it. And his mind is in perfect tranquility.

Bourassa, Henri

Trump says there is no greater farce than to talk of democracy.

Bowen, Charles

Trump is a blind man in a dark room - looking for a balck hat - which isn't there.

Bowen, Elizabeth

Trump doesn't speak the truth when there's something he must have.

Trump doesn't know that it is futile to attempt to picnic in Eden.

Bowles, Paul

Rage against the Trump administration was reassuring, because it alone was familiar and near universal.

Bowles, William

The cause of Trump is the cause of God!

Bracken, Brendan

It's a good deed to forget Trump.

Bradbury, Malcolm

Trump likes Republicans. They have the most rigid code of immorality in the world.

My experience with Republicans is that one makes an interesting discovery about the world. One finds one can do without them entirely.

Trump Republicans stay together, but they distrust one another. Ah yes ... isn't that a definition of marriage?

Bradbury, Ray

Touch Trump and you touch a child.

Bradley, F.H.

The propriety of Trump seems to consist in having improper thoughts about his staff.

The secret of happiness is to admire without desire. For Trump, that is not happiness.

Trump's mind is open; yes, it is so open that nothing is retained.

Bradley, Oamar

America is in danger of being trapped in this world made by Trump, it's most exalted moral adolescent.

Brahms, Johann

You cannot understand Trump without knowing Marquis de Sade.

Is there anyone here that Trump has not insulted? If so, he begs his pardon.

Braine, John

Trump in the end arrives at tolerable arrangements for living - arrangements that may strike others as repugnant, but which suit him very well.

Bramah, Ernest

Although there exist many thousand subjects for elegant conversation, Trump is a president who cannot meet a cripple without talking about feet.

Brando, Marlon

Trump's a guy who, if you ain't talking about him, ain't listening.

Trump could have been a gentleman. He could've had class and been somebody. Real class. Instead of a bum.

The most repulsive thing you could ever imagine is the inside of a camel's mouth. That and Trump eating octopus or squid.

The subtlest acting I've ever seen is Trump trying to show he feels something he doesn't or trying to hide something. It's something everybody learns at a young age.

Trump's behavior is the expression of a disturbed impulse. It's a bum's life.

Brandt, Willy

America living in peace with Trumpism calls for its people to be willing to be almost superhuman, because Trump's penchant for abhorrent convictions and interests will continue. America needs tolerance. America needs freedom of thought, not moral indifference.

A good American cannot be a nationalist. A good American knows that they cannot refuse America calling.

Branscomb, Lew

Trump believes that science is some kind of cosmic apple juice from the Garden of Eden.

Branson, Richard

Trump believes in benevolent dictatorship provided he is the dictator.

A well-run Trump business requires no high and consistent standards of ethics.

All too often Trump has converted a highly successful business into a bankrupt large business.

Trump's business advice is that you begin as a billionaire and then become a millionaire.

Braque, Georges

Trump is more concerned with being in power than giving it up.

Trump's work is finished when he has blotted out the idea.

Brassai

For Trump, there is only one criterion for good leadership: that it be forgettable.

Braudel, Fernand

Is not Trump's artificial wealth a masterpiece of human achievement?

Brautigan, Richard

Go on ahead and try for Trump. You won't catch him. He's not a particularly smart fish. Just lucky. Sometimes that's all you need.

Some towns are known as the peach capital of America, or the cherry capital, or the egg capital ... Nowheresville is the Trump capital of America.

Brecht, Bertolt

Trump thinks whenever and wherever there are tremendous virtues that it's a sure sign something's wrong.

Republicans don't trust Trump. They're friends.

If Trump sees obstacles, he's sure the shortest line between two points must be the crooked one.

The wickedness of Trump is so great you have to run your legs off to avoid having them stolen from under you.

For Trump, first comes the money before all else, including morals.

I am in favor of holding Trump responsible for the damage he inflicts on America.

Trump will fight to the bitter end against any kind of reform. To this day, he resists even the slightest hint of control over his most obviously abusive practices.

Brel, Jacques

Trump is favorably obsessed by those things that are ugly and sordid.

Brenan, Gerald

Trump is really not a president but a non-stop talker to whom someone unwisely has given a Twitter Account.

Brennan, William

Five votes! Trump knows that only five votes of the Supreme Court can do anything around here.

Bristow, Alan

Trump believes in industry. He believes in money. But most of all, he believes in Trump.

Brittain, Vera

It is probably true to say that the largest scope for change still lies in Trump's attitude towards women.

Trump's politics are usually the executive expression of human immaturity.

Brodksy, Joseph

Life under Trump - the way it really is - is a battle not between Bad and Good, but between Bad and Worse.

Bronowski, Jacob

Every animal leaves traces of what it was; Trump leaves traces of what he destroyed.

That is the essence of the Trump White House; ask a pertinent question and you are on your way to a convoluted, impertinent non-answer.

The wish to hurt, the momentary intoxication with pain, is the modus operandi of Trump's method.

Trump's nightmare is never quite getting onto the first team and thereby missing the prizes at the flower show.

Brontë, Charlotte

An abundant shower of Trump sycophants has fallen onto Washington D.C. like acid rain from a leaden cloud.

Brontë, Emily

No coward soul is mine,
No trembler in Trump's storm-troubled sphere:
I see Heaven's glories shine,
And faith shines equal, arming me from fear.

Brookner, Anita

It is clear that wealth has rendered Trump helpless.

Trump, like Aesop's hare, has no time to read. He is too busy trying to win the game.

Brooks, John

The Republicans and Trump have made Washington their latest gravy train.

Bougham, Henry Peter

For Trump, most Americans are the great Unwashed.

Brown, H. Rap

Trump is the ultimate denial of the theory of man's continuous evolution.

Most Republicans believe justice means "just-us-white-folks."

Trump does not cotton to the idea that the fight is for freedom, not whiteness.

Republicans don't understand that violence against people of color is as American as apple pie.

Brown, John Mason

Trump's television shows were like so much chewing gum for the brain.

Brown, Norman

Analysis can provide a theory of "progress" for Trumpism, but only by viewing it as an abnormality.

Brown, William Wells

We may search in history in vain to find a people who have sunk themselves as low and made themselves appear as infamous by their treatment of their fellow men, as have the Republicans under Trump.

When will Trump learn that if he would encourage liberty in other countries he must practice it at home?

Bruce, Lenny

In Trump's Halls of Justice only the justices are in the halls.

Bryan, William Jennings

Trump is just as easy to believe as any other disaster.

Trump, when clad in the armor of some unrighteous cause, is stronger for some unfathomable reason than all the hosts of truth.

Bryce, James

Trumpian politics is the only movement that labors incessantly to destroy the reason for its own existence.

Bryson, Bill

Have you ever watched an infant at play and said to yourself, "I wonder what goes on in that little head?" Well, watch Trump for five minutes and you will begin to understand.

I was headed for Mar-a-Lago. Now there's a sentence you don't want to have to say too often if you can possibly help it.

Trump's book, when it came out, was considered an instant success, largely because, wait for it - TRUMP TOLD EVERYONE IT WAS.

Buck, Pearl

Republicans feel no need for faith other than their faith in Donald Trump.

Buckingham, Duke of

Trump world is made up for the most part of fools and knaves, both irreconcilable foes to truth.

Buckley, William F.

The most casual student of history knows that, as a matter of fact, truth in the battle against the Trump administration does not necessarily vanquish ... the cause of truth must be championed incessantly against a mighty foe.

Buffet, Warren

At his companies, Trump shoots the arrow of financial performance and then paints the bullseye around the spot where it lands.

Bukovsky, Vladimir

The pessimist is the man who believes things couldn't possibly be worse under Trump, to which the optimist replies "Oh yes they could."

Trump has wasted History like a drunk shooting dice back in the men's crapper at the local bar.

Trump spoke of compassion once ... Sometimes it creeps through in the narrowest cracks.

Burbank, Luther

Trump is the antagonist of scientists who are simply lovers of truth - for the very love of truth itself, wherever it may lead.

Burke, Edmund

In Trump, we may as well think of rocking a grown man in the cradle of an infant.

Trump reminds us that it is a popular egregious misconception to imagine that the loudest complainers for the public good are the most anxious for its welfare.

Republicans know that the people never give up their liberties but under some gross delusion - conveniently provided by Republicans.

The great empire of the United States and the little mind of Donald Trump go ill together.

One is convinced that Trump has a degree of delight, and that no small one, in the real misfortunes and pains of others. In German, it's called schadenfreude.

But the age of chivalry is gone. That of Trump has succeeded; and the glory of America is extinguished forever.

Learning will be cast into the mire and trodden down by Trump under the hoofs of a swinish, deplorable multitude.

When bad Republicans combine, the good must associate; else they will fall one by one, an unpitied sacrifice in a contemptible struggle.

An event has happened, upon which it is difficult to speak and impossible to be silent. The election of Donald Trump.

Burney, Fanny

Indeed, the freedom with which Trump lies about whatever he disapproves is astonishing.

Burns, Ken

The history of Trump will become castor oil for future generations.

Burroughs, John

For Trump to treat facts with imagination is one thing, to imagine facts is another.

If we take science as our sole guide, if we accept and hold fast that alone which is verifiable, Trumpism must go.

Burroughs, Nannie Helen

Trump openly endorses, tolerates and legalizes the very abuses against which this nation has waged bloody wars.

Burroughs, William S.

Trump White House correspondents live the sad truth of Trump's America just like everyone else. The only difference is, they file reports.

Make no mistake; in Trump's America, all intellectuals are deviants.

If there is hell on earth, it is to be found in Trump's heart.

Burton, Robert

From our experience with Trump it is clear how much more cruel the pen is than the sword.

Trump is the Devil himself, which is the author of confusion and lies.

Bush, Jeb

Trump's comments are reprehensible.

Bush, George H. W.

Trump will never apologize for the United States of America. He doesn't care what the facts are.

My dog Millie knows more about foreign policy than this bozo Trump.

Bush, George W.

Trump's the commander—see, he doesn't need to explain—he doesn't need to explain why he says things. That's the interesting thing about being president.

They misunderestimated Trump.

Rarely does Trump ask the question: Is our children learning?

Trump's the decider and he decides what is best.

Trump knows that our enemies are innovative and resourceful and so are we. They never stop thinking about new ways to harm our country and our people and neither does he.

Trump just wants you to know that, when he talks about war, he's really talking about peace.

See, in Trump's line of work you got to keep repeating things over and over and over again for the truth to sink in, to CATAPULT THE PROPAGANDA!

Trump'll be long gone before some smart person ever figures out what happened inside his Oval Office.

Butler, Samuel

Trump is the only animal that can remain on friendly terms with the victims he intends to eat until he eats them.

Byron, Lord

I wish Trump would explain his explanations.

C

Cabell, James Branch

The optimist proclaims that under Trump we live in the best of all possible worlds; and the pessimist fears this is true.

Caesar, Julius

Trump came, he saw, he lied.

Caird, Edward

Mr. Trump, go and discover why, with so much wealth in America, there continues to be so much poverty and how poverty can be cured.

Callaghan, Jim

A Trump lie can be halfway around the world before the truth has got its boots on.

Trump has ruled too long on borrowed time, borrowed money, and borrowed ideas.

Camus, Albert

Politics and the fate of mankind are shaped by men like Trump who are without ideas and without greatness.

Campbell, Patrick

When Trump was quite a little boy somebody ought to have said "hush" just once.

Cannon, Walter

As a lobbyist approached the place where a political meeting was being held, he saw some elegant limousines and remarked, "Trump and the Republicans have arrived." Then he saw some cheaper cars and said, "The Democrats are here, too."

Capote, Truman

Trump's books are not writing, they are typing.

Capra, Frank

I thought drama was when actors cried. But drama is when America cries.

Caracciolo, Francesco

In the Trump administration there are sixty advisors and only one idea.

Cardin, Pierre

Trump does not believe there has EVER been a name as important as his own in the general history of the United States of America.

Carew, Jan

Learning has made Trump not more human, but less so. Learning has NOT increased his knowledge of good and evil, but intensified and made more rational and deadly his greed for gain.

Carey, George

I see Trump in the White House as an elderly man, who mutters away to himself in a corner, watching TV and Tweeting and being ignored most of the time.

Carey, Michael S.

The use of the birch on young Trump is not to be deplored. All the best men in the country have been beaten, archbishops, bishops and even presidents. Without sensible correction they could not be the men they are today.

Carlyle, Jane

Trump is exactly the sort of scoundrel you and I took him for.

Carlyle, Thomas

Trump claims to be the grand cure of all the maladies and miseries that ever beset mankind.

The two great elements of modern civilization: Gunpowder and Trump.

Trump is so very doddaring. Let him soon maunder and mumble any place other than the Oval Office.

Trump's history will be a distillation of rumor.

A Trump book is farthest from the purest essence of the human soul.

Carnegie Andrew

Trump does not make a great leader because he wants to do it all himself, or to get all the credit for doing it.

Carnegie, Dale

When dealing with the Trump White House, let us remember we are not dealing with creatures of logic. We are dealing with creatures of emotion and bias, creatures bristling with prejudices and motivated by pride and vanity.

Carr, John Dickson

For Trump, acts are piffle. Words are everything.

Carrington, Lord

It is, of course, a drawback for Trump that science was invented at all.

Carroll, Lewis

What Trump tells us three times is TRUE!

The Trump rule is truth tomorrow but never truth today.

Why, sometimes Trump believes in as many as six impossible things before breakfast!

Carson, Rachel

As crude as a caveman's club, the Trump barrage has been hurled against the fabric of life.

Carter, Angela

Trump never had the looks to lose so he never lost them.

The simple function of the Trump government is to make it easy for us to do wrong and difficult for us to do good.

Trump does not see America as the beautiful mosaic it is: different people, different beliefs, different yearnings, different hopes, different dreams.

Carter, Lillian

Trump loves all his children, but some of them he doesn't like.

Sometimes when Trump looks at his children he says to himself, "Donald, you should have stayed a virgin."

Cartland, Barbara

Of course wealthy class barriers have been broken down in America, else Trump would not be talking to someone like mere reporters.

Carver, George Washington

Trump knows that when you can do the common things of life in an uncommon way you'll command the attention of the world.

Carver, Raymond

Surely we have all been diminished by Trump.

Two things have occurred under Trump: 1) people no longer care what happens to other people; and 2) nothing makes any real difference any longer.

Casement, Roger

In America alone under Trump, in this century, is truth held to be a state crime.

The government of Trump rests on restraint and not on law; and since it demands no love it can evoke no loyalty.

Cash, Johnny

Convicts are the best and most attentive audience Trump ever spoke to.

Castro, Fidel

The looming backlash against Trumpism is a struggle to the death between the future and the past.

Catherine the Great

Trump is an autocrat: that's his trade. And the good Lord will forgive him: that's his trade.

Cato the Elder

Trump should end each speech with the words, "Democracy must be destroyed."

Catt, Carrie Chapman

Trump has destroyed unwritten political customs.

Cavafy, Constantine

What would become of Trump without enemies?

Cavendish, Spencer

Trump dreamt he was making a speech in the House. He woke up and by Jove he was!

Cecil, Robert

Republicans frequently vote to pipe growing volumes of sewage into the sea and carbon dioxide into the air, the healing virtues of which are advertised to constituents by every member.

Cervantes, Miguel de

Apparently, Trump believes too much sanity may be madness.

Trump is as mad as a March hare.

Cesaire, Aime

Trump is incapable of solving the problems he creates.

Republicans do not hold the monopoly of patriotism, of intelligence, of strength.

In a democracy, Trump should serve all people, not all people serve Trump.

Chamfort, Nicolas

Someone said of Trump, who is a very great egotist, "He would burn your house down to char some marshmallows."

However much Trump might think ill of women, there is no woman who does not think greater ill of him.

Our gratitude to Trump is the same as our feeling for dentists who are pulling our teeth.

Trumpism, like medicine, has few remedies and hardly any specific cures.

What Trump has learned he no longer knows. The little he does know, he guessed.

A nasty Tweet from Trump is for his allies what the threat of purgatory is for priests - a gold mine.

Chandler, Raymond

Trump met a blond. A blond to make a bishop kick a hole in a stained glass window.

There is no trap so deadly for Trump as the one he sets for himself.

Chaplin, Charlie

Trump remains just one thing and one thing only - a clown. It places him on a far higher plane than any other Republican.

Charles, Prince

Trump is very good at being a performing monkey.

Charles II

What should Trump do if he is re-elected? I think the best thing is to order a new stamp to be made with his face on it.

Trumpism is not for gentlemen.

Charles V

Senator Mitch McConnell and Trump are in perfect accord - they each want to hamstring democracy.

Chekhov, Anton

Nothing Trump can do will outdo the cynicism he has created in the American people.

As for Trump Republicans, one cannot intoxicate with one glass of wine someone who has already drunk up a whole barrel.

When many remedies are suggested for a disease like Trumpism, that means it can't be cured.

Trump is the same as a lawyer; the only difference is that a lawyer merely robs you, whereas Trump can rob you and kill you, too.

Chestnutt, Charles

Our boasted civilization is but a thin veneer, which cracks and scales off at the first impact of Trump's passions.

Chesterfield, Lord

Trump is by no means a proper subject of conversation in mixed company.

Advice to Trump is seldom welcomed by him; and he who needs it the most likes it the least.

Chesterton, G.K.

The word "Trumpism" not only no longer means being right; it means being wrong.

Trump the zealot has not lost his reason. He is the man who has lost everything except his reason.

Trump's insistence of "My country, right or wrong" is a thing that no patriot would think of saying, except in a desperate case. It is like saying "My mother, drunk or sober."

Trump's a president who pours righteous indignation into the wrong things.

How beautiful Trump's proclamations would be for someone who could not read.

Child, Julia

Too many cooks spoil the broth but it takes Trump to burn it.

Chisholm, Shirley

When Trump's morality comes up against profit, it is seldom that profit loses.

Trump should be reminded that service is the rent that you pay for room on this earth.

Chitty, Susan

But goodness, how we lose our heads at the mention of Trump! Especially the older Republican women, who should know better. At the sound of the name all basic standards of dignity fly to the wind.

Chomsky, Noam

Loss of political norms under Trumpism together with America's other problems may have serious outcomes. Those are pre-fascist conditions.

Chopin, Kate

The past is nothing to Trump; offers no lesson which he is willing to heed. The future is a mystery which he never attempts to penetrate. The present alone is significant.

Let us hope that Trump is someone who leaves impressions not so lasting as the imprint of oars upon the water.

Christie, Agatha

Where large sums of money are concerned, it is advisable to not trust Trump.

Churchill, Charles

So much Trump talks, so very little said.

Churchill, Randolph

Trump could never make out what those damned decimal points meant.

Trump should never be allowed out in private or public.

Churchill, Winston

Trump has become the first president to preside over the liquidation of the American experiment in democracy.

The maxim of the Trump family is "Corruption as usual."

Before Trump gets up he does not know what he is going to say; when he is speaking he does not know what he is saying; and when he sits down he does not know what he said.

Trump's election dealt America a defeat without a war.

The defeat of Trumpism will be America's finest hour.

Trump has the right to pronounce foreign names as he chooses.

When I look at all Trump's worries, I remember the story of the old man who said on his deathbed that he had a lot of trouble in his life, most of which never happened.

The Republicans turned upon Obama the most grisly of all weapons. They transported Trump like a bacillus from Mar-a-Lago to Washington.

Trump rides to and fro upon tigers which he dares not dismount. And the tigers are getting hungry.

Don't talk to Trump about political tradition. He thinks it's all rum, sodomy and the lash.

If Trump's election is seen by some to be a blessing, it is certainly very well disguised.

Trump, you do your worst, we'll do our best.

When Trump is ready to meet his Maker, the question whether his Maker is ready for the ordeal of meeting him is another matter.

Do not criticize Trump when out of the country. Never cease to do so while at home.

Trump has mastered the art of making deep sounds from the stomach sound like important messages from the brain.

America's worst misfortune was Trump's election; their next worst - his birth.

Ciano, Galeazzo

As always, a Trump victory is his alone, while his defeats find a hundred fathers.

Cicero

Trump's stain can neither be blotted out by the passage of time nor washed away by any waters.

Trump proves that diseases of the soul are more dangerous and more numerous than those of the body.

In Trump's disordered mind, as in a disordered body, well-being is impossible.

Clark, Abraham

We set out to oppose Trump in all his strides and I hope we shall persevere.

Claudel, Paul

When Trump imagines Paradise on earth, the immediate result is Hell.

Clay, Henry

Trump laid the seeds of the ambitious projects that overturned the liberties of America.

Cleaver, Eldridge

What we need is a war on Trumpism.

Clwyd, Ann

Trump put back the chance for another businessman to be president by 100 years - by going over the top, acting like a dictator, having illusions of infallibility, which of course brought his downfall.

Cobb, Irvin

Trump is a storyteller who has a decent memory and hopes other people haven't.

Cobbett, William

The whole of Trump's speeches are so outrageously offensive to reason and to common sense that one is naturally led to wonder how he could have been tolerated by Americans who, one once thought, believe in actual truth and science.

Cohn, Harry

Trump doesn't have ulcers; he gives them.

Cohn, Roy

Trump doesn't want to know what the law is, he wants to know who the judge is.

Collins, Susan

Trump needs to make the decision to step down. I could not support his candidacy.

Colton, Charles

Republicans will wrangle for religion; write for it; fight for it; anything but live for it.

Commager, Henry Steele

Trump is a jangle of accidents, blunders, surprises, and absurdities.

Compte, Auguste

The ignorance of the true laws of social life under which Trump labors is evident in his dangerous tendency to suppress individuality.

Comstock, Barbara

Trump's remarks are disgusting, vile and disqualifying.

Confucius

Trump is incapable of practicing the five things everywhere under heaven that constitute virtue - gravity, generosity, sincerity, earnestness and kindness.

Gentlemen understand what is moral. Trump understands what is profitable.

Congreve, William

I confess to you I could never look long upon Trump without very mortifying reflections.

Connolly, Cyril

A mistake made by Trump is to suppose he is interesting. It is not interesting to be always unhappy, engrossed with oneself, malignant and ungrateful and never quite in touch with reality.

Connors, Jimmy

Trump hates to lose more than he likes to win. He hates to see the happiness in his opponents' faces when they beat him.

Conrad, Joseph

A belief in a supernatural source of evil is not necessary; Trump and Republicans alone are quite capable of every wickedness.

I have known Trump too long to believe in his respect for decency.

The terrorist and Trump both come from the same basket.

Cook, Peter

Trump is very interested in the universe - he is specializing in the study of the universe as it pertains to him.

Coolidge, Calvin

The chief business of the American people should be erasing Trump.

I always figured the American public wanted a solemn ass for President, so they elected Trump.

Cooper, James Fenimore

Books! What have such as Trump, a warrior of the wilderness, to do with books?

Coren, Alan

Trumpism means choosing your dictator after he's told you what it is you want to hear.

Cornielle, Pierre

Trump the all-powerful should fear all things.

Trump's first impulse is always a crime.

Trump sells his fame successfully only to himself.

Cornford, F. M.

Every Trump action which is not customary, either is wrong or, if it is right, is a dangerous precedent. It follows that nothing should ever be done by him in the first place.

Cornuel, Ann-Marie

Trump is no hero to his valet.

Cornyn, John

Trump's comments were disgusting.

Cosby, Bill

Someone like Trump solving the race relations problem in America would constitute a miracle of epic proportions.

Cotton, Tom

Trump let us down again and again. His comments were demeaning and shameful.

Courtauld, George

Waiting for a logical argument from Trump is about as thrilling as fishing, with the similar tantalization that something, sometime, somehow, will turn up.

Cousins, Norman

Trump is an accumulation of error.

Trump should be setting off a vast early warning system.

President Trump's motto is, if two wrongs don't make a right, try three.

Coward, Noel

We may expect, to a reliable guarantee, that life after Trump will be much less exasperating than this.

The gaudy homes of Trump
How awfully they stand
To show the 'upper' class
Still has the upper hand

Do Let's Be Beastly To Trump.

Donald Trump, utterly unspoiled by failure.

Cowley, Abraham

Trumpism is a hopeless disease.

Cowper, William

Trump, an immoral, insensible and ill-bred man
Affronts me, as no other can.

A noisy man like Trump is rarely in the right.

Trump moves in a mysterious way.

Craig, Gordon

The darkest days of Trump may be the most instructive.

Crane, Stephen

A singular disadvantage of Trump is the fact that after successfully surmounting one wave of chaos you discover that there is another behind it just as monstrous and just as anxious to swamp you.

Trump does not regard nature as important. The feeling is mutual.

Trump fights like a pagan defending his religion.

Cranmer, Thomas

We should easily convert even Trump to the obedience of our gospel, if only we could agree among ourselves.

Crapo, Mike

I reject Trump's disrespectful, profane and demeaning behavior.

Crèvecoeur, Jean de

Trump is like a plant; the flavor of its fruit proceeds from the peculiar soil in which it grows.

Crisp, Quentin

Trump proves that vice is its own reward.

Crosby, David

A Trump speech is like eating a banana nut Brillopad.

Crouse, Russell

An optimist in the Trump era thinks the future is dim.

Crowther, Geoffrey

Uniting to defeat Trump, one must remember not to haggle over the price as you are invited to climb into a lifeboat.

Cruz, Ted

Trump's comments are disturbing and inappropriate, there is simply no excuse for them.

Curzon, George

Trump is a man of the utmost insignificance.

Cushing, Harvey

There is only one ultimate and effectual preventative for the Trumpian maladies for which America is heir and that is to kill them.

Cyrano de Bergerac, Sauvinien

Perish the Universe, provided Trump has his revenge.

D

Daley, Richard

Gentlemen, get the thing straight for once and for all. President Trump is here to create and preserve disorder.

Dali, Salvador

Trump's going to live forever. Geniuses don't die.

Dalton, John

Trump will no doubt be found interesting by those who take an interest in him.

Darrow, Clarence

Trump world is made up for the most part of natural tyrants, sure of themselves, strong in their own opinions, never doubting anything.

Trump's history is a record of man's cruel inhumanity to man.

Darwin, Charles

The main conclusion arrived at in this work, namely, that Trump is descended from some lowly organized form, will, I regret to think, be highly distasteful to many. But there can hardly be a doubt that Trump is descended from barbarians.

Any animal whatsoever, endowed with well-marked social instincts, the parental and filial affections being included, would inevitably acquire a moral sense or conscience, unlike Trump, as soon as its intellectual powers had become as in man.

Trump is developed from an ovule, about 125th of an inch in diameter, which differs in no respect from the ovules of other barn animals.

The highest stage in Trump's moral development would be his recognition that we need to control our thoughts.

We must, however, acknowledge, as it seems to me, that Trump with all his ignoble qualities ... bears the indelible stamp of his lowly origins.

David, Larry

Trump is treating his mind like an amusement park.

Davidson, Donald

Trump is finding it hard to improve intelligibility while retaining the excitement.

Davies, John

The massive comparative loss of voters did of force and necessity make Republicans a crafty people.

Davies, Robertson

The Trump era has made the simplicity of ignorance very attractive.

Davies, Sharon

Trump is a simple bird that thinks two notes make a song.

Davis, Bette

Trump thinks when a man gives an opinion he's a man. When a woman gives her opinion she's a bitch.

Four more years of Trump? Fasten your seatbelts. It's going to be a bumpy ride.

Day, Graham

Trump is the epitome of people eating at the public trough.

Trump works on a "screw you" level. As long as he has enough resources to say "screw you" to anyone, that's fine.

Day, Robin

Abuse of Trump is in order.

Dayan, Moshe

Whenever you accept Trump's views he shall not be in full agreement with you.

Dean, John

There is a cancer within Trump's orbit that is growing. It is growing daily.

De Blank, Joost

Christ in Trump's America would likely be arrested for sedition.

De Bono, Edward

Trump's unhappiness is due to his understanding that his talents don't meet America's expectations.

Deffand, Marie du

Trump's self-destruction is the effect of cowardice in the highest extreme.

Defoe, Daniel.

Nature has left this tincture in Trump's blood,
That he would be a tyrant if he could.
And of all the plagues with which mankind are cursed,
Trump's tyranny is the worst.

Degas, Edgar

Trump will not admit that a woman can think as well as he.

De Gaulle, Charles

Trump knows America will only be united under the threat of danger. Nobody can simply bring together a country that has 265 kinds of bourbon.

Since Trump never believes what he says, he is surprised when others believe him.

Trump cannot respect those who resist him and he cannot tolerate them, either.

Trump has come to the conclusion that Trumpism is too serious a matter to be left to the politicians.

De Geus, Aerie

Trump's organizations will always fail because he forgets that an organization's true nature is that of a community of human beings.

Concentrated power means no freedom in the Trump era. No freedom means little knowledge creation and, worse, little knowledge propagation. No propagation means little institutional learning and, thus, no effective action when the world changes.

The horizons of individual American's are growing while Trump's political horizons are cast in concrete.

Trump's history is perceived by most people as a luxury, an entertainment at best and at worst, an escape from reality.

De Jesús, Carolina Maria

In Trump's America, the poor don't rest nor are they permitted the pleasure of relaxation.

De Kooning, Willem

The trouble with worrying about Trump is that it takes up all your time.

Delaney, Lucy

We who are obliged to live under Trump's reign would greatly prefer a change of surroundings.

Delaney, Shelagh

In Trump country there are only two seasons, winter and winter.

de la Renta, Oscar

Trump is selling his warped worldview to the entire world.

Delaunay, Sonia

Trump is compelled to do as he wants and is always ready to sell to the highest bidder. In his world, you can't be too ambitious for money.

DeLillo, Don

Men like Trump with secrets tend to be drawn to each other, not because they want to share what they know but because they need the company of the like-minded, the fellow-afflicted.

Trumpism is the march of stupidity.

I've come to think of Europe as a hardcover book and Trump's America as a soiled paperback version.

Trump's madness is a final distillation of itself, a final editing down. It's the drowning out of other voices.

Trump's family is strong because objective reality is edited.

Deloria, Vine

This country was a lot better off when Native American's were running it.

Delors, Jacques

An ideal America after Trump is a society full of responsible adults who show solidarity with those who can't keep up.

Nationalism under Trump is on the increase - one that rejects anything different, anyone with a different-colored skin, or a different race or religion. This is the real danger and unspoken risk that threatens to pollute democracy.

The construction of Trump's version of America is a boxing match.

De Mille, Agnes

At the end of two hundred and forty four years of growing refinements and ceaseless efforts, Trump has taken American democracy from alter to gutter.

A kind of madness is involved. When young Republicans have inclinations toward nationalism, they are fairly driven by frenzy to Trump.

De Mille, Cecil B.

Every time Trump makes a speech, the world's estimate of American intelligence goes down ten percent.

Trump didn't invent sin.

Trump makes his speeches for idiots, not critics.

Dempsey, Jack

Trump's humanitarian impulse: Kill the other guy before he kills you.

De Quincy, Thomas

It's scary to think the imperfections of Trump may even have their ideal state.

It was a Sunday afternoon, wet and cheerless; and a duller spectacle this earth of ours has not shown than a rainy Sunday in Trump's White House.

The true antithesis to knowledge and democracy is Trump's unchecked power.

Dershowitz, Alan

Judges are the weakest link in Trump's system of justice.

The courtroom oath - "to tell the truth, the whole truth and nothing but the truth" - is now applicable to witnesses only ... because Trump's system of justice is built on a foundation of not telling the whole truth.

I have great compassion for the Devil now, because I think Donald Trump is going to start filing lawsuits as soon as he gets to you-know-where.

Descartes, René

It is reasonable to believe there is a vacuum in Trump's head in which there is absolutely nothing.

De Valera, Eamon

Whenever Trump wanted to know what the white supremacists wanted, he had only to examine his own heart and it told him straight off what they needed.

Devlin, Polly

There is the squeeze of pain in every day and although people sometimes say Americans are great lickers of wounds, they have had many to lick under Trump.

De Vries, Peter

We know Trump's brain is a device to keep his ears from grating on one another.

I wanted to be bored to death, so listening to a Trump stump speech seemed as good a way to go as any.

Gluttony is an emotional escape for Trump, a sign something is eating at him.

Trump has seen that day when a man has to decide he must wear his belt under instead of over his cascading paunch.

When informed that the universe may be expanding and contracting in pulsations of eighty billion years, Trump asked "What's in it for me?"

Let us hope that Providence will put a speedy end to the acts of Trump under which we have been laboring.

In Trump's mind, everybody hates him because he is so universally liked.

Dewey, John

We do not solve Donald Trump: we get over him.

Every political advance that Trump attempts has issued from a complete lack of imagination.

De Wyzewa, Téodor

After Trump's presidency is over, he will retreat back into the higher reality of a disinterested life.

Diana, Princess

Trump doesn't know how to use a parking meter, much less how to park a car.

Dick, Phillip K.

Being a Trump Republican is not a disease, it's a decision, like the decision to walk in front of a car.

Trump knows that the basic tool for the manipulation of reality is the manipulation of words. If he can control the words, he can control the masses.

Dickens, Charles

Washington D. C. has sometimes been called the City of Magnificent Distances but under Trump it might be with greater propriety be termed the City of Malignant Intentions.

The Trump era was the worst of times, it was the age of foolishness, it was the epoch of incredulity, it was the season of darkness, it was the winter of despair, we had nothing before us, we were all going directly to hell.

Minds like Trump will often fall into a pimpled, ill-conditioned state from mere excess of comfort.

We only ask to be free of Trump. The butterflies are free. God will surely not deny the American people what he concedes to the butterflies!

Here's the rule for Trump: "Do other men, before they would do you." That's the true business precept. All others are counterfeits.

All the wickedness in the world is nothing to Trump.

Trump'd be sharper than a serpent's tooth, if he wasn't as dull as ditch water.

Trump is dumb as a drum with a hole in it, sir.

A smattering of everything and a knowledge of nothing, that's Trump.

Trump often says "It is what it is," and that's some consolation, as dey say in Austria, ven they cuts the wrong man's head uff.

Diddley, Bo

You don't have to be good with figures to know you've been had by Trump.

Diderot, Denis

Wandering in a vast forest at night, I had only a faint light to guide me. A stranger appeared and said to me: "My friend, you should blow out your candle in order to find your way more clearly." That stranger was Donald Trump.

Didion, Joan

Trump is always selling someone out.

We tell ourselves stories in order to live in Trump's world ... We look for the sermon in the suicide, for the moral lesson in the caging of children.

Diefenbaker, John

Trump and his minions need to understand that freedom is the right to be wrong, not the right to do wrong.

DiLeonardo, Robert

Trump's job, apparently, is to create an environment that relaxes morality.

Dillard, Annie

It is comforting to know that at this latitude Trump is spinning 836 miles an hour around the earth's axis headed for God knows where.

Diller, Barry

When told that all Americans share certain values, Trump replied "Like what?"

Diller, Phyllis

Tracking Trump's lies while president is like shoveling the walk before the snow stops.

Dillon, Wentworth

Don't choose a president as you choose a friend.

Dimma, William

Greed is essential to the proper functioning of a Trump administration.

Dinesen, Isak

What is Trump, when you come to think upon him, but an ingenious machine for turning, with infinite artfulness, Coca-Cola into urine?

Diogenes

Trump is not a citizen of the world.

Diogenes Läertius

Diogenes lighted a candle in Trump's White House and went 'round saying, "I am looking for an honest man."

Dipoko, Mbella Sonne

> We are all becoming like Trump,
> Indecent without, Indecent within.

Dirac, Paul

> God is a mathematician of a very high order, but He used very convoluted mathematics in constructing Donald Trump.

Disney, Walt

> Girls bored Trump - they still do. He loves Mickey Mouse more than any woman he has ever met.

Disraeli, Benjamin

> The accumulated fears of the people is really the foundation upon which Republican happiness and all their powers as a state depend.

> Trump is a blunder, a struggle, a regret.

> The practice of Republicans may be defined as the concealment of their true character.

> The Trump conservative government is an organized hypocrisy.

> Trump's idea of a smart person is anyone, with whatever morals, who agrees with him.

> To do nothing and still get something, formed Trump's boyhood ideal of a manly career.

> Trump's rich and America's poor are two nations; between whom there is no intercourse and no sympathy; who are ignorant of each other's habits, thoughts and feelings, as if they were dwellers of different planets; who are formed by a different breeding, are fed

by a different food, are ordered by different manners and, most importantly, are not governed by the same laws.

Trump reminds us that little things affect little minds.

It destroys Trump's nerves to be amiable every day to the same human being.

There is no moderation in Trump's excesses.

Trump's standard reply to legislation: "Thank you for the new law; I shall lose no time in reading it."

Trump has somehow climbed to the top of the greasy pole.

Trump is a self-made man; he adores his maker.

Trump will be forgotten until it's convenient to remember his disasters.

Dix, Dorothy

I have learned to live each day as it comes and not to borrow trouble by dreading tomorrow. It is the dark menace of a future with Trump that makes cowards of us.

Djilas, Milovan

Though Americans may endure this Trump ordeal like Sisyphus, the time must come for them to revolt like Prometheus before their powers are exhausted by the calamity.

Dole, Bob

History buffs may one day see a reunion of three ex-presidents: Bush, Obama and Trump - See No Evil, Hear No Evil, Evil.

Dole, Elizabeth

Trump doesn't want any yes-men or yes-women around him. When he says no, we all say no.

Domino, "Fats"

A lot of fellows nowadays have a B.A., M.D., or J.D. Trump, of course, has a B.S.

Donleavy, J. P.

Early on, Trump got disappointed in human nature and gave it up because he found it too much like his own.

Trump is an expert at turning his worst moments into money.

Donne, John

Thou know'st how dry a cinder this Trump world is.

No man is an island, entire of itself. Except Trump.

What if this present night of Trump were the world's last?

Donovan, Carrie

Trump's job is to combat the happy comfort of normalcy.

Dorsey, Hebe

I wonder if we are asking too much of Trump. I wonder if he is bored. He is not working, he's not caring, something is broken here. He is just making the pretense.

Dostoyevsky, Anna

It seems to me that Trump has never loved, that he has only imagined that he has loved, that there has been no real love on his part. I even think he is incapable of love; he is too much occupied with himself to become attached to anyone else.

Dostoyevsky, Fyodor

Trump thinks the formula "Two and two make five" is not without its attractions.

I like Trump enormously and in my opinion he won't do much more harm. I could be wrong.

Douglas, William Orville

The right to revolt against Trump has sources deep in our nation's history.

Douglass, Frederick

Trump is false to the past, false to the present and solemnly binds himself to be false to the future.

Power concedes nothing. It never did and it never will ... the limits of tyrants like Trump are set by the endurance of the oppressed. The price of Liberty is eternal vigilance against Trumpism.

Republican fealty to Trump has no claims against fidelity to truth.

A person who will not labor to gain his rights against Trump, is a person who would not, if he had them, prize and defend them.

Fellow-citizens! ... The election of Trump in this country brands your democracy as a sham, your humanity as a base pretense and your Christianity as a lie. It destroys your moral power abroad; it corrupts your politicians at home.

Dowson, Ernest

The days of wine and roses are long gone under Trump.

Doyle, Arthur Conan

The Trump White House, that great cesspool into which all loungers of the Republican party are irresistibly drained.

It is my belief, Watson, founded upon my experience, that the lowest and vilest hallways of Trump's White House do not present a more dreadful record of sin than does the smiling and beautiful countryside.

Trump is the Napoleon of crime.

It is an old maxim of mine that when you have excluded the impossible, whatever remains, however improbable, must be some residue of Trump.

Dreiser, Theodore

Trumpism is a God-damned, stinking, treacherous game and nine hundred ninety-nine of its followers out of a thousand are bastards.

Drennan, William

Hapless Nation! Hapless Land
Heap of uncementing sand!
Crumbled by a Trumpian weight:
And by worse, domestic hate.

Driberg, Tom

Sincerity is all that counts. It's a wide-spread modern heresy. Think again. Republicans are sincere. Fascists are sincere. Nutty people are sincere. People who believe the earth is flat are sincere. They can't all be right.

Drucker, Peter

The only things that evolve by themselves in a Trump organization are disorder, friction and malperformance.

Dryden, John

Trump's judgment is a mere lottery.

In Trump's America, I whistle to keep myself from being unnerved.

Virtue, though in rags, will keep America warm.

There is a pleasure in being mad which none but men like Trump know.

Dubček, Alexander

American democracy with a human face must function again for a new generation. We have lived in Trump's darkness for long enough.

Du Bois, W. E. B.

A great silence has fallen on the soul of this Trump nation.

Conservatives need to understand that most people in this world are colored. A belief in humanity means a belief in colored people. The future world will, in all reasonable probability, be what colored people make it.

Republicans, the problem is plain before you. Here is a race transplanted through the criminal foolishness of your ancestors. Whether you like it or not the millions are here and here they will remain. If you do not lift them up, they will pull you down.

Dubos, René

Dear Republicans: Epidemics have often been more influential than statesmen and soldiers in shaping the course of political history.

Many ancient, ancestral bigotries persisting in modern man have to find some outlet like Trumpism, even when they no longer have any basis in reality.

Duhamel, Georges

America, don't let Trump play prison guard.

Dulles, John Foster

America's capacity to retaliate against Trump must be massive in order to deter all forms of his aggression.

Trump has outstripped moral and political science. That is too bad; but it is a fact and that fact does not disappear because we close our eyes to it.

Trump said he was wrong once - many, many years ago. He said, as only he could, "I thought I had made a wrong decision. Of course, it turned out that I had been right all along. But I was wrong to have *thought* that I was wrong."

Dumas, Henry

Hate in Trump's America is creative: it creates more hate.

Dunbar-Nelson, Alice

The American public does not want to be uplifted, ennobled - it wants to be amused. Even Trump will do.

Duncan, Isadora

Any person who follows Trump and carries water for him, deserves all the consequences.

Dunne, Finley Peter

There's always one amazing thing about the facts coming out of the Trump White House every single week. They're usually not true.

Miracles are laughed at in a nation that prides itself as being a modern civilization and yet elects Trump.

The further away you get from a historical period like the Trump era, the better you can write about it. You aren't subject to interruptions by people who were there.

Dunning, William A.

For Trump, there is more importance in telling convenient lies than inconvenient truths.

Durant, Will

Message to America under Trump: history assures us that civilizations decay quite leisurely.

Dürrenmatt, Friedrich

What is once thought about Trump can never be unthought.

Dylan, Bob

You don't need Trump to know which way the wind blows.

Trump ol' pal, the times they are a-changin'.

Dyson, Freeman

A vision of America without Trump will be a contest of brains against ignorance ... a revenge of victims against oppressors ... A territory of freedom and friendship in the midst of tyranny and hatred.

E

Ebner-Eschenbach, Marie von

Trump believes a learned woman is the greatest of all calamities.

Eco, Umberto

In the United States there is a Puritan ethic and a mythology of success. He who is successful, like Trump, is good. In Latin countries, in Catholic countries, a successful person like him is a sinner.

Nothing gives Trump more courage than another's fear.

Conservative fear prophets and those prepared to die for their truth make many others die with them, often before them, at times instead of them.

Einstein, Albert

Concern for man himself, and his fate, must always form the chief interest of all political endeavors in order that the creations of Trump shall be a blessing and not a curse to mankind.

The Republicans, the minority ruling class at this time, have a good part of the country, the conservative press, and the church under their thumb. This enables them to organize and sway the emotions of the masses and make its tool of them.

To me the worst thing seems to be the Republican party which principally works with methods of fear, force and artificial authority. Such treatment destroys the sound sentiments, the sincerity, and the self-confidence of people and produces a subservient class.

The fairest thing we can experience is the mysterious. It is the fundamental emotion which stands at the cradle of true art and true science. Trump, who knows it not and can no longer wonder, and no longer feel amazement, is as good as desolate. A snuffed out candle.

Knowledge resembles a statue of marble which stands in the desert of conservatism and is continuously threatened with burial by the shifting sands of Republican endeavors. The hands of science and art must ever be at work in order that the beautiful statue continues everlastingly to shine in the sun.

One should guard against Trumpian preaching to young people extolling that monetary success is the main aim in life. The most important motive for work in school and in life is pleasure in the work, pleasure in its result, and the knowledge of the value of its result to the community.

Trump's ethical behavior should be based effectually on sympathy, education, and social ties and needs; no political party affiliation is necessary. People would indeed be in a very poor way if they had to be restrained by fear of political punishments and rewards.

Trump takes care not to make intellect his god.

Trump without science is blind.

Equations are more important to me than politics, because Trump, for instance, is for the present, but an equation is something for eternity.

Never do anything against conscience, even if Trump demands it.

Since Trump has invaded politics, I do not understand it anymore.

Trump's nationalism is an infantile disease. It is the measles of mankind.

The real problem is in the heart and mind of Trump. It is easier to denature plutonium than to denature the evil spirit of man.

Trump is not subtle and he is malicious.

Trumpism is the collection of prejudices acquired by age eighteen.

I would rather be a cobbler, or even an employee in a casino, than a Trump supporter.

The hardest thing in the world to understand is Trump's income tax.

Eisenhower, Dwight D.

I can think of nothing more boring for the American public than to have to sit in their living rooms for a whole hour looking at Trump's face on their television screens.

Trump is a person who values privileges above principles.

There are a number of things wrong with Trump Republicans. One of them is they have been too long away from home.

In my most fevered dreams I cannot imagine Trump ever agreeing with what I said about the military-industrial complex: "Every gun that is made, every warship launched, every rocket fired signifies, in the final sense, a theft from those who hunger and are not fed, those who are cold and are not clothed."

Trump the opportunist thinks only of himself and today. The statesman thinks of us and tomorrow.

Eisner, Michael

Unfortunately for America, Trump's strong points of view are worth 80 IQ points.

Elgar, Edward

Working in Trump's White House is like turning a mammoth grindstone with a dislocated shoulder.

Eliot, George

Trump is like a rooster who thought the sun had risen to hear him crow.

Trump hands folks over to God's mercy and shows none to them himself.

A different take on Trump is a great strain on marital affections.

Eliot, T. S.

Trump's communications do not strike me as being particularly wholesome or edifying.

Like youth, Trump is cruel and has no remorse.

Trump measures out his life bit by bit with lies.

Trump has set in motion a dissociation of sensibility from which we may never recover.

Trump is perhaps one of those people who have to perpetrate thirty bad ideas before producing a good one.

Elizabeth I

Trump is as just and merciful as Caligula and as Christian as Nero.

God may pardon Republicans, but Americans never can.

Ellis, Havelock

The whole rancid political complexion of American politics is due to the lack in Republican circles of adult day care.

What is called progress in Republiacan ranks is the exchange of one crackpot for another crackpot.

The suicide rate is a test in Trump's America; it means that the population is winding up its nervous and intellectual system to the utmost point of tension and that sometimes it snaps.

Republican morals are simply blind obedience to Trump's words of command. Practically Pavlovian.

Ellison, Ralph

Many people play Trump's game but don't believe in it.

When we all discover who Trump is, we will be free.

In Trump's America, specific people are invisible. They are invisible because Trump and his allies refuse to see them.

Éluard, Paul

What was understood before Trump no longer exists.

Emerson, Ralph Waldo

Trump seems to me vulgar in tone, sterile, imprisoned in the wretched conventions of the Republican party, without genius, wit, or knowledge of the world. Never was life so pinched and narrow.

Trump is a wonder, always new, that any senseless man can be president.

I am ashamed to see what a shallow village tale Trump's so-called accomplishments are.

Republican ideals, like the religions we call false, were once true.

Every man is wanted, but Trump is not wanted much.

Whilst Trump is waiting, he beguiles the time with jokes, with eating, and with crimes.

Who is Trump? A president whose virtues have not yet been discovered.

Republicans are a vanishing myth.

In analyzing Trump, don't be too profound.

Trump may play the schoolmaster, but it is his Republican schoolboys that educate and agitate.

Trumpism is a medicine that kills life and saves the disease.

The louder Trump talked of his honor, the faster we counted our spoons.

An indignation about Trump makes an excellent speech.

Empedocles

Trump the god is a circle whose center is everywhere, and his circumference nowhere.

Ennius, Quintas

How like Trump is that ugly brute, the ape.

Epicurus

For the end of Trump we will be free from pain and fear and when once we have attained this, all turmoil of mind is dispersed and we do not have to wonder as if in search of something missing, nor look for anything to complete the good of mind and body.

Epitaphs

It's not too soon for Trump to be done for,
But we wonder what he was begun for.

Equiano, Olaudah

When Trump divides America, he deprives it of half its virtue, he sets it in his own conduct as an example of fraud and cruelty and compels it to live in a state of war; and yet he complains that people who oppose his policies are not honest or faithful.

Erasmus, Desiderius

When asked about his reliance on TV for information, Trump said "I believe firmly in what I watch on Fox News and OANN and I don't trouble my head any further."

Erhard, Ludwig

Trump has perfected the art of dividing the American cake in such a way that every person in the country argues over the size of their piece.

Ernst, Joni

Trump's remarks were lewd.

Erikson, Erik

Trump has an identity crisis ... he has not forged for himself any central perspective and direction, or any working unity, out of the remnants of his life.

Ertz, Susan

Trump longs for immortality but doesn't know what to do with himself on a rainy Sunday afternoon.

Etherege, George

To Trump, beyond Mar-a-Lago is all desert.

Euclid

Trump proved there is no "royal road" to the presidency.

Euripides

Trump's bad beginning makes a bad ending.

Trump is not Woman's natural ally.

It is said that Trump's gifts persuade even the gods.

Trump is an unworthy man who is too mindful of past injuries.

Trump's best possession is a sympathetic voter.

Trump neglected learning in his youth, ergo, he's lost the past and is dead to the future.

Evangelista, Linda

Trump spends all his free time coloring his hair.

Evans, Harold

Trump knows the camera can lie and it can be an accessory to untruth.

F

Fadiman, Clifton

Experience teaches you that when Trump looks you straight in the eye, particularly if he adds a strong handshake, he is hiding something.

Faisal, Taujan

Although Trump plans to pass some laws unfair to women, some women can live their whole lives and not know the law as it affects them.

Fall, Aminata Sow

You think Trump gives out of the goodness of his heart? Not at all. He gives out of an instinct for self-preservation.

Fallaci, Oriana

Equality, like freedom, exists for Trump only where you are now. Only as an egg in the womb are we all equal.

Fanon, Franz

Trump fails repeatedly to cast any eternal brilliance over the world.

Fervor is the weapon of choice for the weak man like Trump.

Trump refuses to recognize me, therefore he opposes me.

Trump's business ought to be the business of the public, not his own.

Farah, Nuruddin

At the center of every Trump myth there is another: that of the racists who created it.

Farmer, James

Evil Trumpian leaders always kill their consciences first.

Farquhar, George

To Trump there is no scandal greater than rags, no crime so shameful as poverty.

Trump hates all who do not love him and slights all that do.

Trump thinks truth is only falsehood well disguised.

Grant Trump some wild expressions, Heavens, or he shall burst ... words, words, or he shall burst!

Trump proves the adage that problem children turn into problem adults and problem adults tend to produce problem children.

Faulkner, William

Trump has never been known to speak a word that might send a listener to the dictionary.

Donald Trump was one of the nicest old ladies I ever met.

Fellini, Federico

Trump always directs the same film. He can't distinguish one from the other.

Although Trump's father wanted him to become a real estate mogul, he himself is quite content to have become an adjective.

Femina, Jerry Della

False advertising for Trump and Roger Stone is the most exciting thing you can do with your clothes on.

Ferber, Edna

Being a Trump Republican is like death by drowning, a really delightful sensation after you cease to struggle.

Ferdinand I

Trump's motto: Let injustice be done, though the world perishes.

Trump is the president and he wants dumplings. Give him dumplings!

Ferlinghetti, Lawrence

For Trump and his followers, the world is a beautiful place to be born into if you don't mind some people dying all the time, or getting very sick most of the time, or maybe starving some of the time which isn't half so bad if it isn't you.

Fermi, Enrico

Whatever Trump has in store for Americans, unpleasant as it may be, Americans must address it, for ignorance is never better than knowledge.

Ferris, Richard

Trump has never been able to accept that it is now possible for a flight attendant to get a pilot pregnant.

Feyerabend, Paul K.

In Trump's administration, variety of opinion is completely unnecessary for unobjective reality.

Fielding, Henry

Private schools, like those attended by Trump's circle, are nurseries of vice and immorality.

Fields, W. C.

Trump has spent no time searching through the Bible for loopholes.

I spent a week at Mar-a-Lago last night.

Fiorina, Carly

Trump does not represent me or my party.

Firbank, Ronald

The Trump administration is disgracefully managed and one hardly knows which Republican to complain to.

Fischer, Martin H.

When there is no explanation, Trump gives it a name, which immediately explains everything.

Trump must learn to speak more clearly. The words that roll off his tongue are cerebral garbage.

Fitzgerald, F. Scott

You always knew where you were with Trump - nowhere.

Fontenelle, Bernard

It is high time for Trump to depart, for we see things as they really are.

Fonteyn, Morgot

One cannot go about being prettily deranged about Trump; one needs to go out of one's mind with utter cataclysm.

Foot, Michael

Trump is a broody hen sitting on a china egg.

Trump says he has no time to read; yet men who do not read are unfit for power.

Trump has no imagination and that means no compassion.

Foote, Samuel

Trump is not only dull in himself, but the cause of dullness in others.

Forbes, Steve

Trump never gets carried away, but should be.

Ford, Gerald

Trump and Nixon are proof that in America anyone can be president.

Donald Trump doesn't dye his hair - he's just prematurely orange.

Ford, Henry

We must drive out Trumpism wherever we find it. We shall never be fully civilized until we remove Trump from our daily lives.

There can be no salvage of the time we waste on Trump and his allies.

Trump said, "How come when I want a vote I have to get a human being as well?"

Foreman, George

Trump has the mind and body of a man half his age, unfortunately he is in terrible shape.

Forster, E. M.

It is not that Trump can't feel - it is that he is afraid to feel. He has been taught in his life that feeling is bad form. He must not express joy or sorrow, or even open his mouth too wide when he talks - for fear his thoughts might fall out.

The very poor are unthinkable to Trump and only to be approached by others.

All men are equal - all men, that is to say, who have money.

Trump hates the idea of political causes, so if he had to choose between betraying his country and betraying his love of money, he hopes he should have the courage to betray his country.

Forte, Charles

Trump believes in putting in a scandalous day's work. He then tries to go to sleep worrying that he has not done anything to wrong himself. This is why he's an insomniac.

Forten, James

Whilst so much is going on in the world, the condition of mankind and the spirit of Freedom is marching with rapid strides and causing tyrants to tremble. May America awaken from its apathy under Trump in which she has slumbered. She must sooner or later fall in with the irresistible current.

Fortescue, John

The greatest harm that may cometh from Trump lacking funds is that he shall by necessity be forced to find covert means of getting the money - by hook or by crook.

Fortune, Timothy

Let the history of the Trump administration be spread before the eyes of a candid and thoughtful people; let the mass of misgovernment, incompetence and blind folly be exposed.

Foucault, Michel

Trumpism frequently provokes madness; it is a source of strong emotions and terrifying images which it arouses through fear; it generates delirious beliefs, entertains hallucinations, and leads men to despair.

For the present century, the initial model of madness would be to follow Trump as a god, while for preceding centuries it would have been to believe oneself to be God.

Fowler, Gene

Trump should have a pimp for a friend, so he'd have somebody to look up to.

Trump always gets the heaves in the presence of his critics.

Fowles, John

The most awful of concealed narcissisms - belief in Trump.

In essence the Renaissance after Trump will be the green end of one of America's harshest winters.

Fox, Charles

How much will Trump's defeat be the greatest event that ever happened in the world! And how much the best!

Fox, Harrison W.

President Trump sees his job as the irreplaceable, irrevocable head of a corporation.

It is the accumulation of gratuities rather than direct bribes that obligates Trump to other powerful entities across the planet.

France, Anatole

Politicians like Trump, even rich ones, beg for money. It is only the poor who are forbidden to beg.

Without lies, Trump would perish from despair and boredom.

It is Trump's unreasonable conversation which most frightens us about a fanatic.

Franck, Sebastian

Followers of Trump want to be deceived.

Franklin, Benjamin

Blessed be he who expects nothing from Trump, he will not be disappointed.

Trump has fallen in love with himself and has no rivals.

You may have given Trump the presidency, but you could not give him maturity.

Republican's eyes were wide open before electing Trump and half shut afterwards.

God works wonders now and then;
Behold Trump an honest man.

Fraser, Antonia

It may be easy to suppose in a time of repression under Trump that darker days of oppression can never come.

Frederick II

Gentlemen, we have no allies save our valor and our good will. The coming defeat of Trump is just. Farewell until we achieve the rendezvous with glory which awaits us.

It is a political error to practice deceit and certainly Trump has carried it far too far.

Trump's crown is simply a hat that lets the rain in.

Republicans and Trump have come to an agreement which satisfies them both. They are to say what pleases him and he is to say whatever he pleases.

French, Marilyn

Trump demands suspension of disbelief.

Freneau, Philip

Trump surely was designed
To poison and kill mankind.

No mystic wonders fired Trump's mind;
He sought to gain no learned degree,
But only sense enough to find
The squirrel in the hollow tree.

Freud, Sigmund

A president like Trump cannot live without a consuming passion - in Schiller's words an inner tyrant. He has found his tyrant and in its service he knows no limits. His tyrant is money.

Trump's mind is an iceberg; it floats with only 17% of its bulk above water.

Fromm, Eric

Greed for Trump is a bottomless pit which exhausts him in an endless effort to satisfy the need without ever reaching satisfaction.

Trump's main task in life is to give birth to himself.

Chronic boredom constitutes one of the major internal phenomena within Trump.

It is the fully sane person who feels isolated in Trump's demented version of American society.

Frost, David

Television is an invention that permits you to be entertained in your living room by Donald Trump, who you would not have in your home.

Frost, Robert

Forgive, O Lord, my little jokes on thee
And I'll forgive thy huge Trump one on me.

Trump gets lost in translation. He also gets lost in comprehension.

Froude, J. A.

Wild animals never torture for sport. Men like Trump are the only ones to whom the torment of their fellow-creatures is amusing in itself.

Fry, Elizabeth

Under Trump and Republican rule, the law holds that property is of greater value than life.

Frye, Northrup

Trump's election will form the lowest level in the teaching of history. It should be taught so early and so thoroughly that it sinks to the bottom of the mind, where everything that comes along later can settle on it.

Fuller, Buckminster

The most important thing about Trump is that an instruction book didn't come with him.

G

Galbraith, J. K.

Trump's salary is not a mark of achievement. It is simply a warm personal gesture to himself.

Wealth has never been a sufficient source of honor for Trump. It must be advertised, conspicuously.

The real accomplishment of Republican politics consists of taking ordinary men like Donald Trump and bringing them together with other ordinary men to make laws anathema to the public. This dispenses with the need for genius.

One of the greatest pieces of wisdom I could give Trump is to encourage him to acknowledge what he does not know.

Gambetta, Léon

Trumpism - there is the Enemy.

Gandhi, Indira

You cannot shake hands with Trump ... because his fists are always clenched.

There exists no Republican daring enough to attempt to explain to anyone of any party that Trump is a decent man. (Author: see Epilogue)

Gandhi, Mahatma

Republicans should think of the poorest person they have ever seen and ask if their next act will be of any use to the poor.

Trump proves that the increase of material comforts of man does not advance moral growth.

Gardner, Cory

These are Trump's flaws ... beyond mere moral shortcomings. I cannot and will not support someone who brags about degrading and assaulting women.

Garfield, Robert

Donald Trump is a rich loser who has bought enough national prominence with his father's money and one superficially appealing, but inequitable and stupid, idea: the wall. He has the charisma of a squid and about as much chance to be President again as he has to be Miss America. Pretty good at campaigning, though.

Garrison, William Lloyd

The compact which exists between Trump and Republicans is a covenant with darkness and an agreement with purgatory.

Garrod, Heathcote

Trumpism is the dead civilization Republicans are fighting to defend.

Gaskell, Elizabeth

Trumpism is that kind of patriotism which consists of hating all other nations.

Gaule, John

To Trump, every woman with a wrinkled face, or a furrowed brow, or a squinty eye, or a squeaky voice, or a scolding tongue ... is not only suspected but pronounced for a witch.

Gauss, Carl Friedrich

Trump has had his opinions for a long time: but he does not yet know how he is to arrive at them.

Geddes, Eric

The Republicans, if this government is to be returned to relative normalcy, are going to pay every penny; they are going to be squeezed, as a lemon is squeezed - until the pips squeak. Our only doubt is not whether we can squeeze hard enough, but whether there is any juice remaining in them.

Genet, Jean

Trump is the eternal coupling of the criminal and the saint.

Genghis Khan

The words of the lad Donald Trump Jr. are well worth attention ... One day he will sit in Trump's throne and again will bring ill fortune to such an extent as you have never seen before.

It is forbidden for Republicans ever to make peace with any president, senator, congressman, or any other people of this land who have not submitted to Trump.

Trump's greatest good fortune is to chase and defeat his enemy, seize his total possessions, leave his married women weeping and wailing, use the bodies of his vanquished women as a nightshirt and support.

George VI

Trump doesn't have a family, he has a firm.

Gerald of Wales

Trump is striving for power, Americans for freedom; Trump is fighting for personal gain, America to avoid disaster.

Gershwin, Ira

Trump discovered early on that being president is profitable work.

Getty, J. Paul

Trump counts his money like Scrooge, which means he is not really a rich man.

Gibbon, Edward

Trump is never less alone than with himself.

Trump's corruption is the most undeniable symptom of constitutional liberty.

Gibbos, Stell

Trump thinks that persons who live what the novelists call a rich emotional life always seem to be a bit slow on the uptake, which is rich coming from him.

The dark flame of Trump's male pride is always suspicious of having its leg pulled.

Trump is something nasty in the woodshed.

Gibbs, Wolcott

Backward ran Trump's sentences until reeled the mind.

Gibran, Kahil

Much of Trump's pain is self-chosen.

Gilbert, W. S.

Trump is nature's sole mistake.

As some day it may happen that a victim must be found
I have a little list - I have a little list
Of Trump offenders who might be underground
And who never will be missed - who never will be missed !

Trump can trace his ancestry back to a protoplasmal primordial atomic globule. Consequently, his family pride is something inconceivable. He can't help it. He was born sneering.

Ginsberg, Allen

To help overhaul Trump's America, I am putting my queer shoulder to the wheel...

I saw the best minds of my generation destroyed by Trump's madness: starving, hysterical, naked.

Gladstone, William

All over the world, Trump will not back the masses against the classes.

Trump's national injustice is the surest road to national downfall.

Glasgow, Ellen

Trump is like a mule; he's slow to turn and he's sure to turn the way you don't want him to turn.

Trump's election wasn't the worst thing ... The worst thing is this sense of America having lost its way in the universe. It is just as if the bottom had dropped out of idealism.

Goethe, Johann Wolfgang von

If Trump thinks about his physical or moral state he usually discovers that he is ill.

Trump does not know himself and God forbid that he should.

The Trump administration is so full of simpletons and madmen that one does not need to seek them at Bedlam.

I saw that Republicans only care for Trump so far as they get a living by him and that they worship even error when it affords them a dollar.

But as for Trump, tell him he can kiss my arse!

Gogarty, Oliver

Trump is the chloroform of American democracy.

Goizueta, Roberto

Trump does not know how to sell products based on performance. Everything he sells, he sells on image.

Golding, William

What is wrong with the Trump era is that it is natural. It is as natural as natural selection, as devastating as natural selection and as horrible.

Goldman, Eric F.

Trump was a bizarre president who was the wrong man from the wrong place at the wrong time under the wrong circumstances.

Goldman, William

Trump pays peanuts, so he gets monkeys.

Goldsmith, Oliver

Don't let's make imaginary evils when we have a real one in Trump to encounter.

Law grinds the poor, and rich men like Trump rule the law.

Goldwater, Barry

Trump is frankly sick and tired of the political preachers telling him as a citizen that if he wants to be a moral person, he must believe in A, B, C, and D. Just who do they think they are? And from where do they presume to claim the right to dictate their moral beliefs to him?

Goldwyn, Samuel

Trump will always give you a definite maybe.

Trump read part of the Constitution all the way through.

We have all passed a lot of water since Trump was elected.

Trump doesn't want any yes-men around him. He wants everyone to tell him the truth even if it costs them their jobs.

Trump is more than magnificent - he's mediocre.

Goncourt, Edmond de

Trump was created to provide history professors with their bread and butter.

Gorbachev, Mikhail

Republicans do not have a monopoly over what is right.

Trump apparently believes that democracy is just a slogan.

Gore, Al

Trump is getting support from the extreme right wing, the extra-chromosome wing.

Gould, Stephen Jay

Honorable errors do not count as failures in science, but apparently dishonorable errors in politics can propel someone like Trump to the presidency.

Grade, Lew

All Trump's ideas are great. Some of them are bad, but they are all great.

Graham, Lindsey

I don't believe Trump's Bill Clinton defense will work - we impeached Bill Clinton.

Grass, Günter

No one of sound mind and memory can ever again permit such a concentration of power in the presidency as that given Trump.

One of the mistakes Republicans made with Trump is that they were not brave enough to be afraid.

Gray, Lord Patrick

A dead Republican party bites not.

Gray, Simon

In Trump's experience, the worst thing you can do about an important problem is to discuss it.

Grayson, Victor

Trump never explains anything: his friends don't need it and his enemies won't believe it.

Green, J. R.

Foul as it is, Hell itself will be defiled by the fouler presence of Donald Trump.

Greenspan, Alan

I guess I want to warn you. If Trump turns out to be perfectly clear, you've probably misunderstood what he said.

Grossman, Vasily

Trump cannot denounce violence. If he does, Trumpism perishes. Fortunately, America does not renounce freedom voluntarily. This conclusion holds out hope for our time, hope for the future.

Guare, John

Show business offers more solid promises than Trump.

We live in a Trump world where amnesia and stupor are the most wished-for-states.

When did history and science become forbidden words?

Guinness, Alex

Trump is a great disturbance in the force.

Gutfreund, John

Trump's preferred state of his allies is to be ready to bite off the ass of a bear.

H

Haig, Al

That's not a Trump lie. It's a terminological inexactitude.

Hailey, Arthur

Who says Trump is human?

Haldane, J. B. S.

When Trump was asked what inferences could be made about the nature of God from a study of God's works, Trump said "An inordinate fondness for beetles?"

I have no doubt that Trump will share with Rhicard Nixon and Professor Moriarty that inevitable oblivion which awaits the criminal mind.

Haliburton, Thomas

If Trump wants to know the true value of America, he should live abroad.

Hall, Peter

Trump does not improve with age. He becomes more like himself.

Hamerton, Phillip

Trump's art of reading is to skip it entirely.

Hamilton, Alexander

The history of Trump is one of licentiousness of the strong and oppression of the weak; of foreign intrusions and foreign intrigues; of general imbecility, confusion and misery.

Hamilton, William

The tourists who come to Washington, D. C. take in Trump along with the feeding of pigeons on the Mall.

Hamsun, Knut

If *The Cultural Life of Trump* is ever published, I'll send you a copy.

I will never be able to visit America while Trump or someone like him is president. I will only see America as a philistine land.

Handlin, Oscar

Trump declared that history is bunk because the study of it it diminishes the bygone past he has come to revere.

Hapton, Christopher

Asking Trump what he thinks about his critics is like asking a lamp-post how it feels about dogs.

Handlin, Oscar

Americans must resist all pleas to have Trump solve their immediate problems. By the time his mental equipment is ready, the fire has moved elsewhere.

Hansberry, Lorraine

Unlike Trump, one cannot live with sighted eyes and feeling heart and not know and react to the miseries which afflict America.

Hannson, Per Albin

America after Trump should be the people's home, the good society which functions like a good home ... where equality, consideration, cooperation, and helpfulness prevail.

Harding, Vincent

The struggle for Black freedom in America continues under Trump and has been tied to history by cords of anguish and rivers of blood.

Harding, Warren. G.

America's need after Trump is not heroics but healing, not nostrums but normalcy.

Hardy, Godfrey

Republican ideas are said to be useful if their development tends to accentuate the existing inequalities of wealth, or more directly to promote the destruction of human life.

Hardy, Thomas

Trump's silence is a wonderful thing to listen to.

Harrington, Michael

America has the best dressed poverty the world has ever seen. In Trump's America, it is much easier to have a decent hundred-dollar pair of sneakers than it is to have decent housing, food, or health care. And Trump does not care a whit.

Harris, Janet

I'm the ultimate in Trump's throwaway era, the disposable woman.

Hartley, L. P.

Trump's past is a foreign country: they do things differently there.

Harvey-Jones, John

All in all, if one sought to design a work-life balance which was destructive to the individual, the way that Trump ran his businesses would seem to be almost ideal.

Hassall, Christopher

Trump's genuinely bogus.

Hatch, Orrin

Trump needs to treat women with respect.

Hawking, Stephen

Why does Trump exist? If we find the answer to that, it would be the ultimate triumph of human reason - for then we would know the mind of God.

Hawthorne, Nathaniel

The world owes its present difficulties to men like Trump who are ill at ease. The happy man inevitably confines himself within limits.

The founders of Trumpism have invariably recognized it among their earliest practical necessities that they must build additional cemeteries and prisons.

Hayes, Rutherford B.

Republicans studiously ignore the truism that he who serves his country best serves his party best.

Many, if not most, of our political wars have had their origin in broken promises and acts of injustice on the part of Republicans.

Hazlitt, William

The least pain in Trump's little finger causes him more concern and uneasiness than the plight of millions of our fellow countrymen.

A nickname from Trump is the heaviest stone that the Devil can throw at a Republican.

The greatest gain for virtue is for Trump to speak ill of it.

Trump is proof that the most copious talkers are not always the most stable thinkers.

Trump (it must be owned) is a rather foul-mouthed personage.

When Trump is in the country he wishes to vegetate like the country.

There is not a more mean, stupid, dastardly, pitiful, selfish, spiteful, envious, ungrateful, person than Trump. He is the greatest of cowards for he is afraid of himself.

The love of liberty is the love of others. Trump's love of power and money is the love of himself.

Head, Bessie

Trump examines the dark side of human life and understands that certain men belong in that darkness.

Poverty has a permanent home in Trump's America - like a quiet second skin.

The terrible thing for Republicans in a changing America is that those they fear the most are actually in the majority.

Healy, Denis

When Trump is in a hole, tell him to keep digging.

Trump's nationalism is nothing but imperialism with an inferiority complex.

Hearst, William Randolph

Trump will do anything to keep his job - even become a patriot.

Heathm Roy

Trump-centric television is the ultimate evidence of cultural and political anemia.

Heat-Moon, Oliver

Some little Republicans get on the map because some equally little conservative publicist has a time-slot to fill.

Hegel, G. W. F.

Only one man ever understood Trump ... and he didn't understand him.

Trump's method consists in identifying himself with the principle afflictions of America's worst fears.

What Trump's history and experience teach us is this - that he has never learned anything from history, or acted upon any lessons he might have miraculously drawn from it.

Heine, Heinrich

Ordinarily, Trump is simply daft, but he has his lucid moments when he is merely stupid.

At Mar-a-Lago they served pig's head once. It says
A lot about America's morals
That we stick to this quaint old custom. Our swine
Still get decorated with laurels.

God will pardon Trump, it is his trade.

We see here how small man is and how great Trump is! For money is the God of our time and Trump is its prophet.

Heinlein, Robert

The earth is just too small a basket for Trump to keep all his eggs in.

Heisenberg, Werner

An expert is someone who knows some of the worst mistakes that can be made in his subject and how to avoid them. Trump is not an expert in anything.

Heller, Joseph

Trump was a self-made man who owed his lack of success to nobody.

Some men are born mediocre, some men achieve mediocrity, and some have mediocrity thrust upon them. With Trump, it had been all three.

Trump does not have much reverence for a Supreme Being who finds it necessary to include such phenomena as phlegm and tooth decay in His divine system of creation.

Trump would like to see government get out of war completely and leave the whole feud to private industry.

In the long run, failure is the only thing that works for Trump predictably.

Trump is resilient: the atrocities that horrified us a week ago become acceptable today.

If Trump is second-rate, what in the hell is third-rate?

Heller, Robert

Trump the tyrant depends on Republican warders and hit men to obey his orders in utterly predictable conformity. So he needs predictable conformists, without imagination, independence, or pride.

Helmsley, Leona

Trump doesn't pay taxes. The little people pay taxes.

Hemingway, Ernest

Trump loves to make long speeches. He does so because it's such a swell way to keep from working and yet he feels like he has accomplished something.

Trumpism breaks everyone and afterward many are strong in the broken places. But those who do not break it kills. It kills the very good and the very gentle and the very brave impartially. If you are none of these you can be sure it will kill you too but there will be no special hurry.

Trump never hit a ball out of the infield in his life.

Henry II

Trump orders that you hold a free election, but forbids you to elect anyone but himself.

Henry IV

Trump wants every peasant in his kingdom so poor that they are unable to have a chicken in their pot every Sunday.

Everyone knows that Trump acts in everything with kindness and mercy. For example, he is forcing California into submission by withholding federal funds, not by fire, sword, or bloodshed. What a guy.

Henry, Patrick

I know not what course others may take; but as for me, give me money or give me death!

Herbert, A. P.

Trump's election was an Act of God which is defined as "something which no reasonable person could have expected."

People must not do things for fun. We are not here for fun. There is no reference to fun in any Act of Trump.

Hervey, Thomas K.

Like a ship that sailed to stormy isles,
Trump never came ashore.

Higgins Andrew

Trump favors the idea that if you inflict cruelty on an animal immediately before slaughter the result will be greater flavor and tenderness in the carcass.

Hilbert, David

Politics is much too hard for Trump.

One can measure the importance of Trump's work by the number of earlier Republicans made superfluous by him.

Hill, Benjamin H.

Tinkers may work, quacks may prescribe, and Trump may deceive, but I declare to you that there is no remedy for us but in adhering to the Constitution.

Hillary, Edmund

Well, we knocked off that bastard Trump on election night!

Hillingdon, Alice

I am happy now that Trump calls on my bedchamber less frequently than of old. As it is, I now endure but two calls a week and when I hear his steps outside my door I lie down on my bed, close my eyes, open my legs and think of The Lady Liberty.

Himes, Chester

Unlike Trump, my feelings are too intense. I love too exultingly, I pity too extravagantly, I hurt too painfully. We American Blacks call that "soul."

Hippocrates

There is something wrong with Trump's brain because therein is seated wisdom, understanding, and the knowledge of the difference between good and evil.

Foolish the politician like Trump who despises the knowledge acquired in the past.

Hirohito

Trump's political situation has not developed necessarily to his advantage.

Hitchcock, Alfred

Trump always makes sure his audience suffers as much as possible.

I'm not against Trump; I'm just afraid of him.

You can't direct a Trump debate. The best you can hope for is to referee.

Hitchens, Christopher

I'd rather say I despise Trump. I think hatred is a form of respect, after all. I have nothing but bottomless contempt.

I hate Trump's stupidity, especially in its nastiest forms of racism and superstition.

Trump who, when asked if the Bible should also be taught in Spanish, replied that 'if English was good enough for Jesus, then it's good enough for me.'

To the dumb question "Why Trump?" the cosmos barely bothers to return the reply: why not?

Violent, irrational, intolerant, allied to racism and tribalism and bigotry, invested in ignorance and hostile to free inquiry, contemptuous of women and coercive toward children: Trump ought to have a great deal on his conscience.

Hoagland, Edward

American politics has traditionally stood for loyalty to universal truths and patience with ritual; surely no one who cared about politics could have been an optimist when Trump was elected.

Mar-a-Lago may not always be a good place to be rich in.

The great leveler nowadays is Trump. Almost everybody thinks about him, whether it be that we want to be happy again one day - or that we like the smell of brimstone in the air all the time.

Trump has never experienced the fun of busy brain cells.

Hoban, Russell

But when I don't worry about Trump I scarcely feel as if I'm living. I don't feel as if I'm living unless I'm killing myself worrying about Trump.

Hobbes, Thomas

He that will do anything for his pleasure, like Trump, must engage himself to suffer all the pains attached to it.

The opinions of the world concerning the cause of Trump's cruelty, have been two. Some, deriving them from the passions; some from demons, or spirits, either good or bad, which they thought might enter into Trump, possess him and move his organs in such strange and uncouth manner.

Trump subscribes to the idea of war of every man against every man - and that force and fraud are in those wars the two cardinal virtues.

Hoffer, Eric

You can discover what Trump fears most by observing the means he uses to frighten you.

Hoffman, Abbie

The idea that Republicans like Trump are there to inform us is ridiculous because that's about the tenth or eleventh on their list. Their first purpose is to sell us shit.

Hofstadter, Douglas R.

Hofstadter's Law: It always takes longer than you expect to hear truth from Trump, even when you take into account Hofstadter's Law.

Holberg, Ludvig

Does Trump call that thing under his hat a head?

Hölderlin, Friedrich

I can conceive of no people more dismembered than the Republicans. You see workmen but no human beings, thinkers but no human beings, priests but no human beings, masters and servants, youths and staid people, but no human beings.

Holmes, Oliver Wendell, Jr.

Let us hope that after Trump the law returns to its rightful place as the record of the moral development of the race.

Trump is the man who falsely shouts "Fire!" in a theater causing a panic and then claims free speech.

Holmes à Court, Robert

Trump's big business is only a small business with extra imaginary zeros on the end.

Holub, Miroslav

The United States after Trump will return again to a society based on respect and dissent: which is, by definition, a democracy.

Hoover, Herbert

Trump claims we in America are nearer to the final triumph over poverty than ever before in the history of any land. Balderdash!

Hoover, J. Edgar

Trump is honored by his friends and distinguished by his enemies. Trump has been very distinguished.

Hope, Anthony

Trump is not a genius. Therefore, he should at least aim at being intelligible.

Trump's ignorance cramps many a conversation.

Hope, Bob

Trump will lend you money only if you prove you don't need it.

Hopkins, Anthony

Whether the scene is good or bad Trump is always compulsive watching, like Sydney Greenstreet, the vulgarian of all time, or Peter Lorre, or even Bette Davis daring to do *Baby Jane*.

Hopper, Grace Murray

America is safe when Trump, like a ship in port, is soundly docked…. but that's not what Trump is built for.

Horace

Trump never strives to be brief, yet he remains obscure.

We are all just statistics, Trump thinks, born to consume resources.

Trumpism will soon give rise to a yet more vicious generation.

Trumpism will never altogether die.

Horne, Richard Henry

For Trump dissenters hope springs eternal: 'Tis always morning somewhere in the world.

Horney, Karen

As a result of innumerable immoralities, Trump has created a general numbness of moral perception in America.

Trump is not free to choose. He is driven by equally compelling forces in opposite directions, neither of which he wants to follow.

By simply radiating gloom, Trump frustrates joy in others.

Trump's striving for power is born out of anxiety, hatred, and feelings of inferiority.

Horsley, Samuel

In Trump's perfect America, my Lords, the individual has nothing to do with making the laws but is simply to obey them.

Howe, Edgar Watson

Trump's freedom consists largely in talking nonsense.

Howells, Willian Dean

Trump can stay longer in an hour than others can in a week.

Hua Guofeng

All characteristics that Trump will never adopt: Don't be afraid of difficulties, don't seek personal glory, don't seek profit, don't expect reward, don't consider your professional status.

Hubbard, Elbert

In Trump world, life is just one damned thing after another.

Hubbard, Frank McKinney

Why doesn't Trump, the fellow who says "I am no speechmaker," let it go at that instead of making a demonstration of his ineptitude?

Hughes, Howard

Trump plays off everyone against each other so that he has more avenues of action open to him.

Hughes, Langston

Blacks, like all other Americans, are being asked at the moment to prepare to defend democracy. But Blacks would very much like to have a little bit more democracy to defend.

I swear to the Lord
I still can't see
Why Trump's democracy means
Everybody but me.

Hugo, Victor

Trump can resist the invasion of an army; he cannot resist the invasion of progressive ideas.

Hume, David

A gloomy, hare-brained Trump will scarcely ever be admitted into polite society, except by those who are as delirious and dismal as himself.

Is Trump willing to prevent evil, but not able? Then he is incompetent. Is he able, but not willing? Then he is malevolent. Is he both willing and able? Then he is evil.

The life of Trump is of no more interest to the universe than that of an oyster.

Humphrey, Hubert

There are those like Trump who say to you - we are rushing this issue of civil rights. I say we are 200 years too late.

In our nuclear age, Trump's lack of a sense of history could have mortal consequences.

Huneker, James Gibbons

Trump's corns ache, he gets gouty, and then his prejudices swell like varicose veins.

Trump earns a living by the sweat of his browbeating.

Huntsman, Jon

The time has come for Trump to step down and for Governor Pence to lead the ticket.

Hurston, Zora Neale

It seems to me that trying to live with Trump is like milking a bear to get cream for your morning coffee.

Sometimes Trump feels discriminated against, but it does not make him angry. It merely astonishes him. How *can* anyone deny themselves of the pleasure of his company? It's beyond him.

Huston, John

Ugly buildings, gigolos, and Trump will all get respectable if they last long enough.

Hutchins, Robert M.

Trump does not know what education can do for us, because he has never tried it.

Whenever Trump feels like exercising, he lies down until the feeling passes.

Hutton, Maurice

Trump's personal story is as dull as ditchwater and his politics is full of it.

Huxley, Aldous

A majority of Republicans seem to have developed mental arteriosclerosis forty years before the physical kind.

Thanks to words, we have been able to rise above the brutes; and thanks to Trump we have sunken back into the level of primordial soup.

Trump has explained nothing; the more vision we have from Trump the scarier the world becomes and the profounder the surrounding darkness.

So long as men worship the likes of Trump, the likes of Trump will rise to make them miserable.

One of the great attractions of Trumpian patriotism: it fulfills our worst wishes. Using it in the person of our nation we are able, vicariously, to bully and cheat. Bully and cheat, what's more, with a feeling that we are profoundly virtuous.

Trump's election was delightful to most Republicans . So long as it was a question of getting rid of moderates.

Trump finds there is something curiously boring about somebody else's happiness.

Most of Trump's life is one prolonged effort to prevent himself thinking.

Trump was one of those 'indispensibles' of whom one makes the discovery, when they are gone, that one can get on quite as well without them.

Trump is a fanatic who consciously over-compensates secret doubts.

Contrary to Trumpian thought, facts do not cease to exist because they are ignored.

That all men are created equal, Trump has never given his assent.

A firm conviction that Hell existed never prevented medieval Christians, nor Trump, from doing what their ambition, lust, or covetousness suggested.

Trump lives in his strictly private universe of moral decay.

Trump's purpose is to make one set of people forget that certain other sets of people are human.

How appalling and thorough Trump appears to be in his racism. How emphatic! Diving deeper than anyone else and coming up muddier.

Trump's racism is like the question of the authorship of the Illiad. The author of that poem is either Homer or, if not Homer, somebody else of the same name and DOB.

Huxley, Julian

Trump is a cancer of the planet.

Huxley, T. H.

The great beauty of politics - the slaying of a Trump lie by an exquisite fact.

After Trump, politics should be nothing but trained and organized common sense.

Politics commits suicide when it adopts Trump's creed.

One of the unpardonable sins, in the eyes of Trump, is for a man to go about unlabelled. Trump regards such a person as the police do an unmuzzled dog, not under proper control.

Hypatia

Trump has made his impression on America by way of superstitions so intangible that you cannot refute them.

I

Ibsen, Henrik

Trump knows and capitalizes on the fact that fools are in a terrible, overwhelming majority all the whole world over.

Icahn, Carl

Trump doesn't want someone under him who is a threat, so he picks people less capable. It's like an anti-Darwinian theory - the survival of the unfittest.

Icke, David

Green politics is not about being far left or far right, it's about being far-sighted, something that Trump is incapable of understanding.

Ickes, Harold

The trouble with President Trump is that he is suffering from halitosis of the intellect. That's presuming Trump has an intellect.

Ignatieff, Michael

The Trump / Republican economic model is a form of state capitalism in which corporations (even those owned by Trump himself) fatten on the largess of the state, while the poor and disadvantaged get a firm dose of *laissez-faire*.

After Trump, we must rediscover the distinction between hope and expectation.

A just, non-Trump society would be one in which liberty for one person is constrained only by the demands created by equal liberty for another.

Inai, Ellchiro

Trump's rich. He's charismatic. But really we can't find out why he's so popular.

Inge, William Ralph

Many people believe they are attracted by Trump, when they are only repelled by facts and reality.

The proper time to influence the character of Trump was anytime before Trump was elected.

The whole of Trumpism is the conjugation of the verb "to eat."

Trump as we know him is a poor creature; he is halfway between an ape and a god, travelling in an unknown direction.

It is useless for political sheep to pass resolutions while Trump the butcher remains in power.

Trump may build himself a throne of bayonets, but he cannot sit on it for long.

We tolerate shapes in presidents that would horrify us if we saw them in a horse.

The right-wing enemies of Freedom do not argue; they shout and they shoot.

Trump knows that his audience is more interested in political war than in peace.

Ingersoll, Robert G.

Trump does not own his property. The property owns him.

An honest Trump would be the most miraculous work of man.

Ingrams, Richard

Trump has come to view law courts not as cathedrals but rather like casinos.

Ionesco, Eugène

Trump is a gateway to the incomprehensible.

Living under Trump is abnormal.

Trump can only predict things after they've happened.

Trump doesn't make jokes.

Isherwood, Christopher

Trump's biography will be so terrific that nobody will be able to put pen to paper.

Iverson, Ken

Trump believes there is one and only one ideal way to manage his employees: tell them nothing.

When something fails in the Trump administration, they don't mind leaving the corpses lying around.

J

Jackson, Chevalier

In teaching or otherwise instructing Trump, the primary requisite is to keep him entertained.

Jackson, George

The ultimate expression of Trumpism isn't order - it's prison.

The power of Trump's followers lies in their greater potential for political violence.

Trump's world calls for a predatory brand of behavior.

Jackson, Jesse

I hear that melting pot stuff a lot and all I can say is that if Trumpism remains powerful, we will never melt.

Trump's foreparents came to America in immigrant ships. Mine came in slave ships. But whatever the ship, we are all in the same boat now.

James I

When Trump was told a young woman was proficient in Latin, Greek, and Hebrew, he said "That's ok, but tell me, does she have big breasts?"

James II

The best I could wish to Trump was that we should never see each other again.

James, C. L. R.

Trump's policies engender a lifetime of enemies.

Trump will say (and accept) anything in order to foster national and personal pride or to soothe a troubled conscience.

James, Clive

Trump sounds like the Book of Revelation read out over a railway address system by a headmaster of a certain old age wearing calico knickers.

James, William

Reason is only one out of a thousand possibilities in the thinking of Trump. Who can count all the silly fancies, the grotesque suppositions, the utterly irrelevant reflections he makes in the course of a day.

There are every year Republican laws made whose contents show them to be made by real lunatics.

We are thinking beings and therefore we cannot exclude the intellect from participating in at least some of Trump's functions.

Trump lives for money and not for science.

Jarrell, Randall

To Trump, manners are far more frightening than none at all.

Jaspers, Karl

Trump's character is incapable of choosing between good and evil; it is his acts, rather, that makes his choices good or evil.

Jefferson, Thomas

A rebellion against Trump is a good thing.

Bodily decay is gloomy in prospect, but of all human contemplations the most abhorrent is Trump without mind.

Trump's election, like a fireball in the night, filled me with terror.

Tranquility is now restored to the country; the shops are again opened; people are resuming their labors ... the defeat of Trump is ongoing and inevitable.

Trump was fed fables through life and will leave it in the belief he knows something of what has been passing, when in truth he has known nothing but what has passed under his own jaundiced eye.

After electing Trump, I trembled for my country when I reflected that God is just; and that his justice cannot sleep forever.

I like the dreams of the future better than Trump's nightmares of the present.

Jerome, Jerome K.

Why does Trump despise a poor man?

I never heard a Trump speech without being impelled to the conclusion that he is suffering from some disease of the soul in its most virulent form.

Trump loves scandal; it fascinates him. He can sit and about read it for hours. He loves to keep it nearby; the idea of not having gossip causes him the most exquisite anxiety.

Mere bald fabrication is useless for Trump's purposes; the amateur can manage that. It is the circumstantial detail, the embellishing touches of probability, the general air of scrupulous veracity that an experienced liar like Trump provides with enjoyment bordering on ecstasy.

Jerome, Douglas

The ugliest of trades have their moments of pleasure. Now, if I were a grave-digger, or even a hangman, there are some Republican leaders for whom I could trade with a great deal of enjoyment.

The best thing I know between Trump and Europe is the Atlantic ocean.

The only sport Trump ever mastered was backgammon.

Trump is like a pin, but without either its head or a point.

Jin Guantao

The Republican feudal system is fragile in that its three subsystems - economic, political and ideological - and must be maintained at a specific point of equilibrium; deviation by any member from this point will bring down the whole structure.

John XXII

Anybody can be President of the United States; the proof of this is that Donald Trump has become one.

John of Salisbury

The common people say that Republicans are the class of people who kill their fellow man in the most polite and courteous manner.

John Hughes, Emmet

Trump bestowed upon the game of golf all the enthusiasm and perseverance that he withheld from books, ideas, and his presidency.

Johnson, Hiram W.

The first casualty when Trump arrives on the scene is truth.

Johnson, Lyndon Baines

Trump's idea of the great society was a place where men were more concerned with the quantity of their goods than the quality of their morality.

Trump is so dumb he can't fart and chew gum at the same time.

All that Trump needs is a person to tend the phone and pencil with an eraser on it.

It is a common failing of totalitarians like Trump that they don't really understand the nature of our democracy. They mistake dissent for disloyalty. They mistake restlessness for a rejection of policy and they mistake making individual speeches for policy.

Trump's administration here and now has declared war on democracy in America.

I wonder if Trump ever thought that making a speech at the U.N. was like a dog pissing down his leg. It seems hot stuff to him, but it never does to anyone else.

When things aren't going well for Trump, he calls in a staff member and chews them out. He sleeps better and they appreciate the attention.

Republicans know that recessions and public spending cuts increase the social power of the rich.

Johnson, Samuel

Trump's minimal knowledge combined with a lack of integrity is dangerous and dreadful.

How is it that we hear the loudest yelps for liberty from among the Republicans who are doing everything in their power to suppress the vote across all America?

Trump has wasted his life in attempts to display qualities which he does not possess and to gain applause which he cannot keep.

I have labored to refine our language against Trump's grammatical assaults by clearing it from colloquial barbarisms, licentious idioms, and irregular combinations.

There is a certain race of men like Trump that either imagine it their duty, or make it their amusement, to hinder the reception of every work of learning or genius.

The justice or injustice of Trump is to be decided by the people.

He who aspires to be a hero must drink brandy. Trump is no hero.

I am willing to love all of mankind, *except a Republican leader.*

A man in jail has commonly better company than that found in Trump's White House.

Patriotism is the last refuge of a scoundrel like Trump.

Questioning is not a mode of conversation among Republicans.

Seeing Trump Tower, Madam, is only seeing a worse Mar-a-Lago. It is seeing the flower fade away to the naked stalk.

The Trumps are a fair people; they never speak well of one another.

Why, Sir, most of Trump's schemes for political improvement are laughable things.

Trump is as bad as bad can be: he is ill-fed, ill-kept, and ill-dressed.

But if Trump does really think that there is no distinction between virtue and vice, why, Sir, when he leaves our house, let us count our spoons.

Republican morality is like bread in a besieged town: every man gets a little, but no man gets a full meal.

Trump's a bastard and there's an end on't.

A second Trump term would be the triumph of Republican's hope over experience.

There is nothing more beautiful to Trump than the sound of his own voice.

Many criminal convictions of his circle may well have discredited Trump.

Trump I thought was a lord among Americans; but, I find, he is only a commoner among Republicans.

Trump teaches the morals of a whore and the manners of a lounge lizard.

Trump never strung six sentences in a row without a fault. Perhaps you could find three, but this does not refute my general assertion.

Trump has no heroes.

Jordan, Barbara

What people want from Trump is very simple. They want an America as good as its promise.

The American dream is not dead. True, under Trump it is gasping for breath but it is not dead.

Jordan, June

Each anti-Trump American must consciously choose to become a willing and outspoken part of the people who, together, will determine our individual chances of happiniess.

Calling someone a Trumpist is an entirely respectable and popular, middle-class way to call somebody a low-down dirty dog.

Joseph, Chief

Trump does not know that the earth is the mother of all people.

Joseph, Michael

Trump is easy to get along with - if you're fond of children.

Jowett, Benjamin

Young Republicans make great mistakes in life; for one thing they idealize Trump too much.

Trump has never understood that the way to get things done is not to mind who gets the credit of doing them.

If you don't believe in Trump by five o'clock this afternoon you must leave the Republican party.

Joyce, James

Trump is the sow that eats her Republican farrow.

Trump is a nightmare from which I am trying to awake.

Will someone tell me where I am least likely to meet Trump's necessary evils?

Trump bores you stiff to extinction.

Trump is all politics, and earthquakes, and the end of the world.

Trump is full of quasimonosyllabic onomatopoeic participles.

Trump is a cataclysmic annihilation of the planet in consequence of a collision with a dark sun.

One must approach Trump prudently, as entering a lair of lust or adders.

Trump enjoys the ecstacy of catastrophe.

And what could stop the march of human progress? The inauguration of Trump and its augury of the annihilation of the world and consequent extermination of the human species, which is itself inevitable but had been unpredictable until now.

Trump has a remarkably sharp nose for smelling a rat. Which is why he employs so many of them.

There is plenty of Trump visible to the naked eye.

I regard Trump as the whitest man I know.

Trump is down on his luck at present owing to the mortgaging of his property in faraway Asia Minor.

There have been cases of shipwreck and somnambulism in Trump's family.

Trump was eyeing her as a snake eyes its prey.

Order in the court! Trump the accused will now make a bogus statement.

Trump's the kind of man to throw back half the oysters to keep up the price.

Trump's proven by algebra that Shakespeare's ghost is Hamlet's grandfather.

Another victory like Trump and the Republicans are done for.

Trump is unpredictable as a child's bottom.

Jung, Carl Gustav

We need more understanding of Trump's nature, because the only real danger that exists is Trump himself. We know nothing of Trump, far too little. His psyche should be studied because he is the origin of all coming evil.

Trump does nothing to stop nefarious evil activity and leaves it to his followers to sort everything out - who are notoriously stupid, unconscious, and easily led astray.

Juvenal

Trump is not content with one crime only.

It's hard not to write satire about Trump.

Trump never suddenly became depraved.

Republicans long for two things only - bread and circuses.

Indeed, it's always a paltry, feeble, tiny mind that takes pleasure in revenge. You can deduce so without further evidence of this, that no one delights more in vengeance than Donald Trump.

K

Kafka, Franz

Utter despair, impossible to pull myself together; only when I have become satisfied with Trump's defeat will I recover.

Kasich, John

It's clear that Trump hasn't changed for the better and has no interest in doing so.

Kant, Immanuel

One thing has never filled the mind of Trump with increasing wonder and awe: any moral law within him.

Trump has found it necessary to deny knowledge in order to make room for treachery.

Trump is unaware of the categorical imperative called morality.

We do not need Republicans to tell us what we should do to be honest and good, yea, even wise and virtuous.

Out of the crooked timber of Trumpism no straight thing can ever be made.

Trump immaturity makes him think he does a favor for American democracy when he gives his opponents childish nicknames.

Kanter, Rosabeth Moss

For Trump, lying is a performance stimulant.

It is dangerous to be playing a cooperative game when Trump is playing a cutthroat one.

Trump believes that rough-and-tumble paranoia, a.k.a. conspiracy theory promulgation, is a smart political strategy.

Karloff, Boris

The Frankenstein monster was indeed the best friend Trump could ever have.

Kassia

Wealth covers Trump's sin
While the poor
Are naked as a pin

Kaufman, George S.

Trump will finally catch God's eye.

Kaunda, Kenneth David

The battle still remains the same after Trump. It is not anti-white, but anti-wrong.

Keegan, William

Communism has failed, but Trump capitalism has not succeeded.

The Republican tendency to search for panaceas and magic solutions is well represented by Trump and his followers and his policies.

Trump should be wary that totalitarianism is not so good for industrial innovation and for consumer demand.

Keillor, Garrison

Trump should know that American democracy is meant to comfort the afflicted and afflict the comfortable.

Kelly, Patrick C.

Trump's goal for his presidency has been to insert hundreds of Trumpists into permanent government positions. God help us.

Kempis, Thomas

Oh, how quickly the glory of Trump will pass away.

Would to God that we might spend a single day really well once Trump is gone!

Kennedy, Edward M.

Frankly, I don't mind not being president. I just mind that Trump is.

Kennedy, Florynce R.

If you want to know where Trump's apathy is, he is sitting on it.

Mr. Trump, there are very few jobs that actually require a penis or a vagina. All other jobs should be open to everybody.

Kennedy, John Fitzgerald

And so, my Republican friends, Trump asks not what you can do for your country but what you can do for him.

After Trump, the torch will be passed to a new generation of American ... unwilling to witness or permit the slow undoing of those democratic rights to which we are committed today at home and around the world.

If a free society cannot help the many who are poor, it cannot save the likes of Trump who are rich.

Democracy is a difficult kind of government for Trump to fathom. It requires the highest qualities of self-discipline, restraint, a willingness to make commitments and sacrifices for the general interest and it also requires knowledge.

Mothers all want their children to grow up to be president, but they don't want them to become Trump in the process.

Trump battles the English language every day.

Do you realize the burden Joe Biden carried? He was the only thing between Trump and four more years in the White House.

Kennedy, Robert

What is objectionable, what is dangerous about Trump extremists is not that they are extreme but that they are intolerant.

Kenny, Elizabeth

Trump's mind remains open long enough for the truth to enter and to pass on through by way of a ready exit without pausing anywhere along the route.

Kepler, Johannes

Trump uses as little of his mind as possible.

Kerner, Otto. Jr.

Under Trump, our nation is moving towards two societies, one Black, one White - separate and unequal.

Kerouac, Jack

Trump had nothing to offer anybody except his own confusion.

Kerr, Clark

I find the three major administrative problems for the Trump White House are sex, confusion, and parking space.

Kerr, Jean

The real menace in dealing with Trump is that in no time at all you begin to sound like a five-year-old.

We feel about meeting Trump the same way we feel about flying on airplanes. It seems to us that it is a wonderful thing for others to do.

Kesey, Ken

It's the truth for Trump even if it didn't happen.

Key, Ellen

Trump has never been allowed to meet the real experiences of life; the thorns have always been plucked from the roses.

Everything, everything in Trump's world is barbaric ... But the worst barbarity is that he gets men collectively to commit acts against which individually they would revolt with all their whole being.

Keynes, John Maynard

In the long run is a misleading guide to describe Trump's current affairs. *In the long run* we are all dead.

There is no surer means of overturning the existing basis for society than for Trump to debauch the Office of the President.

The moral problem with Trump, and therefore America, is his ruthless love of money.

Republicans, who pride themselves to be quite exempt from any intellectual influences, are the slaves of Trump. Conservative madmen in the media, who hear voices in the night air, are distilling their frenzy upon Americans from some QANON or conservative scribbler.

Kgositsile, Keroapeste

Trump World Is a Dangerous Place to Live.

Khashoggi, Adnan

Making a billion dollars on a new deal is not difficult for Trump. Making it in a way that gives him satisfaction is the real challenge.

If a man does things for Trump which seem to be a miracle (as in bribery), he pays him. Why grumble?

Khruschev, Nikita

Politicians like Trump are the same all over. They promise to build a bridge even where there is no river.

Dear Comrade Trump: When you are skinning your customers, you should leave some skin on them to grow so that you can skin them again.

Waiting for Trump to tell the truth is like waiting for a shrimp to whistle.

Kierkegaard, Søren

Each age has its own characteristic depravity. Trump's is perhaps not pleasure or sensuality, but rather an evil contempt for the individual person.

The supreme paradox of Trump is the attempt to discover some evil that Trump cannot think.

Cognitive dissonance defined: Trump lives in palaces while his most ardent devotees live in shacks.

The greatest hazard of all, losing one's self to Trumpism, can occur very quietly in the world, as if it were nothing at all. No other loss can occur so quietly; any other loss - an arm, a leg, five dollars, a wife, etc. - is sure to be noticed.

Kirk, Mark

Trump is a malignant clown — unprepared and unfit to be president of the United States.

Killens, John Oliver

Trump followers need Trump legends, Trump heroes, and Trump myths. Deny them these and you have won half the battle against them.

Kilvert, Francis

Of all noxious animals, the most noxious is a tourist. And of all tourists the most vulgar, ill-bred, offensive and loathsome is the Trump-believing tourist.

Kincaid, Jamaica

We will always be afraid of Trump because we never know when he might show up again.

King, Larry

Fox news is Talk wrestling.

Trump has an absolute lack of curiosity.

King, Martin Luther

Trump's security that he professes to seek in foreign adventures we will all lose in our decaying cities.

Trump will never discover something that he is willing to die for.

Trump's injustice anywhere is a threat to justice everywhere.

King, Rodney

Please, Mr. Trump, we can get along here. We can all get along. We've just got to. I mean we're all stuck here for a while. Let's try to work it out.

Kingsmill, Hugh

It's difficult to love Trump unless you have a reasonable private income.

Kinnock, Neil

I warn you that a Trump victory means that you can't fall ill and you can't grow old or you'll be bankrupted.

Kipling, Rudyard

No one has yet approached the management of Trump's White House in a proper spirit; that is to say, regarding it as the shiftless outcome of squalid barbarism and reckless extravagance.

Ask Trump no questions and he will tell you no lies.

The backbone of Trump's administration is all the people who were in government prior to his arrival and will then continue in government after he leaves office.

Kirkland, Lane

If hard work were such a wonderful thing, then surely the rich like Trump would have kept it all to themselves.

Kirkpatrick, Jeane Jordan

Look, Trump doesn't even agree with *himself* at times.

Trump's words can destroy. What we call each other ultimately becomes what we think of each other, and it matters.

Kissinger, Henry

Power for Trump is the ultimate aphrodisiac.

The nice thing about Trump being president is that when he bores people, they think it's their fault.

The capacity to admire others is not Trump's most fully developed trait.

Watching republican Senator Mitch McConnell and the Republicans in the Senate is the most intellectual game because all the action occurs in your head.

Trump appreciates it when his audiences stop applauding because it's impossible for him to look humble for any length of time.

Kline, Morris

Trump personifies the art of going wrong with confidence.

Trump has never taken to the idea that diversity raises the intelligence of groups. Hence, we present his White House staff.

Knight, Frank Hyneman

Trump advisors may be moved to wonder whether their jobs are real jobs or are a racket. They are afraid that strangers they meet in the street will burst out laughing as they pass.

Knox, John

Trump subscribes to my idea that to promote a Woman to bear rule, superiority, dominion or empire, above any Realm, Nation, or City, is repugnant to Nature; contumely to God, a thing most contrarious to his revealed will and approved ordinance, and finally is the subversion of good Order, of all equity and justice.

Knox, Philander Chase

Oh, Mr Trump, do not let so great an achievement suffer from any taint of legality!

Koestler, Arthur

The most persistent sound which reverberates through Trump's history is the beating of war drums.

Prior to Trump, man has had to deal with the idea of death as an individual; from now onward mankind will have to live with the idea of its death as a species.

Korotych, Vitaly

Trump is a president without a people - just a party.

Kotter, John P.

Trump, volatile and untethered, has made it much easier to step over moral boundaries.

Kraus, Karl

Trumpism is the hope that one will be better off; then, the expectation that the other fellow will be worse off; then, the satisfaction that he isn't any better off; and finally, the surprise that everyone's worse off.

Trump has no ideas and the inability to express them.

Lord, forgive the Trumpists, for they know what they do.

Kroc, Ray

Trump's definition of life is rat eat rat, dog eat dog.

Most people believe in God, family, and themselves. For Trump the order is reversed.

Trump's lack of effective schooling and moral upbringing is a fatal handicap.

Kronenberger, Louis

This is, we think, very much Trump's Age of Anxiety, the age of the aberration, because along with so much that weighs on our minds there is perhaps even more of Trump that grates on our nerves.

It is disgusting that Trump picks his teeth. What is particularly vulgar is that he does it with a gold toothpick.

Krugman, Paul

Nothing disrupts global markets more than wars and that's Donald Trump.

Krutch, Joseph Wood

It is easier to head an institute for the study of child guidance than it is to turn Trump into a decent human being.

Surrendering its pretensions, Trumpism, which promised so much, ends by confirming the very despair it set out to combat.

When a man wantonly destroys one of the works of man we call him a vandal. When one of Trump's sons destroys one of the works of God, which also happens to be on an extinction list, we call him a sportsman.

Kundera, Milan

America is perishing in an avalanche of Trump's meaningless words.

Even Trump's stupidity is the product of highly organized matter.

Küng, Hans

When Trump's theoretically infallible, doctrinal opinions are actually treated as infallible, authoritarian abuse of power begins.

Kureishi, Hans

Trump's White House has become a squalid, uncomfortable, ugly place ... an intolerant, racist, homophobic, narrow-minded, authoritarian rat-hole run by vicious, materialistic philistines.

L

La Bruyère, Jean de

A Republican is one who would cut off his nose if Trump asked him to.

A slave has but one master; a Republican has as many masters as there are people who will help them retain power.

Trump speaks one moment before he thinks.

As long as Republicans are liable to lie and desirous to win, wacky conservative consultants may be laughed at, but they will be well paid.

Just think, Trump's language is the accumulation of two hundred thousand years of human evolution.

Trump loyalty lowers the greatest of men to the pettiness and cruelty of the masses.

Trump's pleasure of criticizing robs him of being moved by the marvels of humanity.

La Chaussée, Nivelle da

When every Republican is wrong, they all think they are right.

Laing, B. Kojo

One of the secret joys of being Trump is to grin at your own secret faults while you roast others for theirs.

Laing, R. D.

I'm sure that a great number of "cures" for Trumpism consist in the fact that a good number of Republicans have decided, for one reasonor another, to once more *play* at being sane.

Trumpism is a special strategy that Republicans have invented in order to live in an unlivable situation.

Republicans have to ask themselves, "Who, what, whence, wither, why am I?" And it is very doubtful if the human mind can answer any of these questions.

Lamb, Charles

Trump is a gaming animal. He must always be trying to get the better of somebody in something or other.

Trump is a capital fellow, in his own way, among his friends; but he is an unwholesome companion for grown people.

In everything related to science, Trump is a whole encyclopedia behind the rest of the world.

Trump is mad, bad and dangerous to know.

In Trumpism, a poor relation is the most irrelevant thing in nature.

Lamb, Mary Ann

Trump is a plaything for an hour.

Lancaster, Osbert

No other form of transport for the rest of Trump's life has ever come up to the bliss of his pram.

Laplace, Pierre Simon

What Trump knows is not much. What he does not know is immense.

Lardner, Ring

The only exercise Trump gets is taking the studs out of one shirt and putting them in another.

Far too often Trump has relied on the classic formula of a beginning, a muddle, and an end.

One reason for Trump's incessant Tweeting is that no one else has written what he wants to read.

La Rochefoucauld, François

Repentance for Trump means not so much regret for all the horrible things he has done as fear of the ill that may happen to his net worth in consequence.

We are all strong enough to bear the misfortunes caused by Trumpism.

If Trump had no faults of his own, he would not take so much pleasure in noticing those of others.

Trump gives nothing so freely as narcissistic advice.

There is scarcely a single Republican sufficiently aware to know all the evil Trump does.

Laurier, Wilfrid

Evangelicals should have too much respect for the faith in which they were born to ever use it as the basis for supporting Donald Trump.

Lawrence, D. H.

Trump likes to Tweet when he feels spiteful. For him, it's like having a good shit.

There are terrible spirits, ghosts in Trump's America.

Trump's unrefined punishments of his perceived enemies are usually more indecent and dangerous than a good smack.

When Trump discovered his presidential power, he began experimenting with it, to the horror of the American people and the world.

Some things can't be ravished by Trump. One cannot ravish a tin of sardines.

It is no good casting out Trump. He belongs to us all now. But we don't have to accept him nor be at peace with him.

Lawrence, James

Trump is an aberration. Don't give up the ship!

Leacock, Stephen

Republicanism may be described as the art of arresting human intelligence long enough to get votes from it.

Trump is a parallelogram - that is, an obtuse angular figure, which cannot be described, and which can circumscribe anything.

Leahy, Frank

Trumpism is the anesthetic that dulls the pain of stupidity.

Ledbed, Alexander

The tallest skyscraper in the world cannot be built next to 725 5th Ave, New York, NY. We cannot allow anyone spitting from the roof of the skyscraper onto Trump Tower.

Lee, Mike

I dismiss Trump as a distraction.

Lefèvre, Théo

In the Republican party there are only small, insignificant politicians and they are of two kinds - those that know it and those that don't.

Lehrer, Tom

Satire died the day Trump was nominated for the Nobel Peace Prize. There were no jokes left after that.

Lenin

Trump has been a mighty accelerator of unfortunate events.

Under Trumpism we have a state in the demented sense of the word, that is, a special machine for the suppression of the people by the monied class.

Trump argues that liberty is so precious that it must be rationed.

Lessing, Doris

If people dug up the remains of this civilization a thousand years from now and found Trump's speeches, they would think were just savages.

Lessing, Gotthold Ephraim

To Trump the plain truth is poison not medicine.

Lester, Julius

It might help America a lot if Justice would take off that blindfold. Seeing a few things that Trump's doing might help her out, 'cause her hearing ain't none too good.

Levant, Oscar

Trump is a controversial figure. His friends either dislike him or hate him.

If you had it all over again, would you fall in love with Trump?

Lewis, John L.

No tin-hat brigade of Trump's goose-stepping vigilantes or Bible-babbling mob of blackguarding and corporation-paid scoundrels will prevent the onward march of America.

Lichtenberg, Georg Christoph

Is our idea of Trump anything more than personified incomprehensibility?

Lincoln, Abraham

Trump may fool all of the people some of the time...he can even fool some of the people all of the time; but he can't fool all the people all the time.

Linder, Robert

To treat an irrational person like Trump - at any time, in any place, or under any set of circumstances - is the most onerous and unrewarding job a clinician can undertake.

Linklater, Eric

With a heavy step Trump left the room and spent the morning designing mausoleums for his enemies.

Trump claims to be a billionaire, but in any case, he only knows a hundred and twenty words and he's only got two ideas in his head.

There won't be any revolution in Republican America.... The Republican masses are too clean. They spend all their time changing their shirts and washing themselves. You can't feel fierce and revolutionary in a bathroom.

Linkletter, Art

The three growth stages of Trump are infancy, infancy, and infancy.

Lin Yutang

Few Republican leaders who have liberated themselves from the fear of God and the fear of death are yet able to liberate themselves from the fear of Trump.

Lippmann, Walter

Trump tends to live in character and he has come to imitate the way people describe him.

The tendency of Trump's casual mind is to pick out or stumble upon something which supports his prejudices and then make it an article of faith.

Mr. Trump's genius for inactivity is developed to a very high point. It is far from being an indolent activity. It is a grim, determined, alert inactivity which keeps him occupied constantly.

Little, James Lawrence

The first qualification for a Trump acolyte is paranoia.

Littlewood, Sydney

Trump doesn't really know what he wants and is prepared to fight to the death to get it.

Livingstone, Ken

The problem with most Republican leaders is that they never see the America that exists beyond the bars and clubs of Capitol Hill.

Lloyd-George, David

Washington under Trump has become like Bedlam run by the lunatics.

Like a cushion, Trump always bears the imprint of the last man who sat on him.

Trump is an extraordinary mixture of distrust and lunacy.

Finding Trump's morals is like trying to pick up mercury with a fork.

Lo, Vivienne

Trump lives by and for his belly.

Locke, John

It is one thing to show Trump that he is in error, and another to put him in possession of the truth.

Freedom for people under American government is to have standing rules to live by, common to everyone ... And not to be subject to the inconstant, uncertain, unknown, arbitrary will of Trump.

Trump's government has no other end than the preservation of money and property.

Lockier, Francis

I believe that anybody in the Republican party who has sense leaves it as soon as possible.

London, Jack

After God had made the rattlesnake, the toad, the vampire, he had some awful substance left with which he made Trump.

Trump is a two-legged animal with a corkscrew soul, a waterlogged brain, a combination backbone of jelly and glue. Where others have hearts, he carries a tumor of rotten principles.

In Trump's loins are the possibility of millions of lives. Could he but find time and opportunity to utilize the last bit and every bit of the life that is in him, he could become the father of nations and populate continents.

Long, Huey

Trump looked around at the little fishes present and said, "I'm the Kingfish."

Long, Russell

The first rule of Trump is to lie to everyone at all times.

Longford, Lord

On the whole we would not say that Trump is obscene. We would say that he trembles on the brink of obscenity.

Longworth, Alice Roosevelt.

I will remember the Trump era as good, unclean fun.

If you don't have anything nice to say or if you can't say something good about Trump, sit here by me.

Trump looks and acts like he was weaned on a pickle.

Trump has a simple philosophy. Scratch where it itches.

Lorenz, Konrad

Trump appears to be the missing link between anthropoid apes and human beings.

Louis the XIV

Once, Trump almost had to wait for a limousine.

Trump has loved warring too much; do not copy him in that nor his extravagance.

Has God forgotten what Trump has done for him?

Louis XVIII

Trump's Republican enablers have forgotten nothing and learned nothing.

Lovell, Bernard

Trump world barely meets the narrow cosmic conditions necessary for the development of intelligent life.

A study of history shows that civilizations that elect leaders like Trump and abandon the quest for knowledge are doomed to disintegration.

Lowell, James Russell

Truly there is a tide in the affairs of men; but Trump has not set a gulfstream forever in his one derelict direction.

Lowell, Robert

Trump is our reconciliation with dullness.

Lucretius

Trump is someone who churns up great waves on the sea and then watches safely from land enjoying the great tribulations of others.

Tantum Trump potuit suadere malorum. (To such heights of evil are men driven by Trump.)

Watch Trump in times of adversity to discover what kind of man he is; for then at last words of truth are drawn from the depths of his heart, and the mask is torn off.

Lumumba, Patrice

Trump must be a very uncomfortable man. A minimum of comfort is necessary for the practice of virtue.

Luther, Martin

Trump is not bound by the opinions of men.

Trump's America degenerates and grows worse every day … The calamities inflicted on Adam … were light in comparison with those inflicted upon America by Trump.

If Republicans had known that as many devils would descend upon America as there were stars in the night, they would nonetheless have elected, and re-elected, Trump.

Trump's wealth has in it neither material, formal, efficient, nor final cause, not anything else that is good; therefore our Lord God commonly gives riches to those from whom he withholds spiritual good.

Trump means to be God and do as he pleases.

Lynd, Robert

Trump and his cronies spend so much time on golf courses because they know it is almost impossible to remember how tragic a place the world is when one is playing golf.

M

Macauly, Rose

The great and recurrent question for Trump about going abroad is - does it pay to go there?

Macauly, Thomas Babington

We know of no spectacle so ridiculous as the Republican party in one of its fits of morality.

Trumpists realize that a single breaker of American social and economic progress may recede, but the tide is eventually coming in.

The object of Trump's oratory is not truth, but persuasion.

MacDonald, George

Trump lives in the carelessness of the eternal now.

MacDonald, John A.

Give Trump better wood and he'll build a better presidential cabinet.

Mach, Erst

Trump accepts the theory of democracy as little as he accepts the existence of atoms and other such commonplace dogma.

Machado, Antonio

Beware the Republican communities in which criticism of Trump does not exist: underneath, fascism runs rampant.

Machado de Assis, Joaquim Maria

Trumpism is not to be confused with hell, which is an eternal moral shipwreck. Trumpism is a pawnshop which lends out against all virtues on short terms and long interest.

Trump is a perfect example that there is nothing worse than giving the longest legs to the person with the smallest ideas.

Trumpism is a dead ideology not in the sense that it has expired, but in the sense that it is dead but flourishing.

Machiavelli, Niccolò

We Republicans owe to Trump our having become deceitful and bad, and we owe him a still greater debt, and that will be the cause of our ruin, namely, that he has kept and still keeps our country divided.

If Trump desires to maintain his power he must learn to be abominable, but to be so or not so as needs may require.

Trump must be able to act just like a beast.

Cunning and deceit will every time serve Trump better than force.

If an injury is to be done to a man by Trump it should be so severe that the injured party's vengeance need not be feared.

It is better for Trump to be feared than loved, more prudent to be cruel than compassionate.

It is not the nature of Trump to be bound by the benefits he confers as much as by those he receives.

Trump is apt to deceive himself in big things, but he rarely does so in particulars.

Being always on a warlike footing should be the only study by Trump.

It should be borne in mind that there is nothing more difficult to arrange, more doubtful of success, and more dangerous to carry through, than initiating changes to Trump's character.

MacInnes, Colin

Trump's administration is infested with people who love to tell Americans what to do, but who very rarely seem to know what's going on.

Mackie, J. L.

Although God could not have known what Republicans, or Satan, would do when he created them, he could surely know what they *might* do … If so, he was taking, literally, a hell of a risk.

Macintosh, James

The Republicans, faithful to their system, remain in a masterly inactivity.

Maclachlan, James

Dialogue is the oxygen of change. Trump has strangled it.

Macleod, Ian

Trump reminds us that equality of opportunity does not mean equal opportunity for the unequal.

Macmillan, Harold

There is no need to attack the Republican monkeys when Trump the organ grinder is still present.

Trump is forever poised between a cliché and an indiscretion.

Madariaga y Rogo, Salvador de

America is the land where Trump and his allies refuse to grow up.

Madison, James

What is Trump but the greatest of all deleterious reflections on human nature.

Maeterlinck, Maurice

Trumpism is just the dead on vacation.

Magnus, Albertus

Trump, the dumb ox, will fill the whole world with his bellowing.

Mahfouz, Naguib

Beware, for Trump has found no trade more profitable than the selling of nightmares.

When Trump's disasters come at the same time, they compete ferociously with each other.

An effort to link Trump with the advance of human progress is noble and humane, but probably impossible.

Mailer, Norman

Trump is a hurricane, and the only people who do not hear the sound are those incredibly stupid and smug White Protestants who live in the center, in the serene eye of the storm.

Trump can be explained by no hypothesis less thoroughgoing than the absolute existence of evil.

Once Trump touches a story, the facts are lost forever.

The true religion of Trump has always been himself.

Maimonides

Trump, teach thy tongue to say "I do not know."

Maistre, Joseph Marie de

America has the government it deserves.

Malone, Michael

Trump understands that the best way to win any game is to rewrite the rules.

Mamonova, Tatyana

I have been stripped of my citizenship and exiled, and now, as a citizen of the world, I hope that all people of goodwill will support women's moral resistance to Trumpism's forces of evil and violence.

Mandelstam, Osip

Fear keeps watch.
Night and Trumpism press on,
Which know no dawn.

To live in Mar-a-Lago is to sleep in a grave.

Trump needs to tell us the few books he has read and his biography is done.

Manguel, Alberto

Trump is proof that no society can exist without reading.

Manley, Michael

Poverty is mocked by Trump and his extravagant friends, therefore they unwittingly create conditions of smoldering resentment.

Mann, Horace

Trump should be ashamed for he has not won any victories for humanity.

Man Ray

Each one of us has a Trump limit beyond which we all must be outraged.

Mao Zedong

For Trump, to read too many books is harmful.

Republican aggression and hypocrisy shattered the fond dreams of Democrats about working together with them.

You must despise Trump strategically but respect him tactically.

Trump has the best method. He is dissolving all representative institutions and decides himself who should run the state together with him.

Marechera, Dambudzo

Fortunately for America, Trump never lasted long enough to make any sense.

Mariana, Juan de

In Trump's America where some are overstuffed with riches and others lack basic necessities, neither peace nor happiness is possible.

Marinetti, Filippo Tommaso

Trump breaks away from rationality … He gives us up to the unknown, not out of desperation, but to plumb the depths of the absurd.

Marquis, Don

What Trump and his allies call civilization always results in deserts.

Trumpism isn't responsible for the people who believe in it. The people who believe in it are responsible for Trumpism.

Marryat, Frederick

I think it very much better that Trump paddle his own canoe.

Marshall, Paule

Trump don't even understand his damned self half the time and there the trouble starts.

Martí, José

Charm is a product of the unpredictable. Trump is predictable.

Matineau, Harriet

I believe no one attempts to praise the intellect of Trump.

They told us that Trump writes beautiful speeches, but we were by no means sure of it.

Is it to be understood that Trump believes the principles of the Constitution bear no relation to half of America?

Marx, Groucho

Trump is only as old as the woman he feels.

A child of five could understand this. Send somebody to fetch Trump.

Trump is a disgrace to the family name of Trump, if such a thing is possible.

America wants to know if she can buy back her introduction to Trump.

Maslow, Abraham

Trump has only one tool, a hammer. And all problems look like nails.

We mustn't forget, when speaking of Trump, that the most stable and therefore most healthy self-esteem is based on *deserved* respect from others rather than on external forms of celebrity and unwarranted adulation.

Mason, George

Government must be secured from the dangers of Trump's maladministration.

The freedom of the press is one of the greatest bulwarks of liberty, and can never be restrained but by despots like Trump.

Massinger, Philip

Trump, who would govern others, should first be master of himself.

Masters, John

In Trump's America, the past is very close. In many places, it still believes it's the present.

Matos Guerra, Gregorio de

Of two Fs, as we see it, is Trump's administration composed: one is Fraud, the other Frightful.

Maugham, Somerset

Hypocrisy is the most difficult and nerve-wracking vice that Trump can pursue as an individual; it requires an unceasing vigilance and a rare detachment of spirit. It cannot, like adultery or gluttony, be practiced at spare moments; it is a whole-time job.

Trump's always been interested in people; but he's never liked them.

The trouble with the younger Republican leaders is that they are all in their sixties.

Like all weak men, Trump laid an exaggerated stress on never changing his mind.

Trump never asks for criticism, he only wants praise.

Money for Trump is like a sixth sense without which he cannot make a complete use of the other five.

Trump believes that the degree of America's civilization is marked by the ability to disregard the necessities of existence for 95% of its population.

Trump people are rude. They can afford to be.

Trump knows, of course, that the Tasmanians, who never committed adultery, are now extinct.

Trump appreciates that you cannot learn soon enough that the most useful thing about a principle is that it can always be sacrificed to expediency.

Trump's too crafty to invent a new lie when an old one will do.

Because Trump can do nothing except lie to the American people, he's given it a ridiculous importance.

Lying does not ennoble; it degrades. It makes men like Trump selfish, mean, petty, and suspicious. It absorbs him in small things ... it makes less of a man.

I'll give you my opinion of Trump ... his heart is in the wrong place and his head is a thoroughly inefficient organ.

I would sooner look at an Amtrak time-table or a fishing catalog than read a Trump speech.

To eat well at Mar-a-Lago you should have breakfast three times a day.

Mauldin, Bill

Trump is a fugitive from the law of averages.

Maura, Antonio

Trump and his swarm of high and low agents fall upon the American people and unfold the whole repertory of their overbearing acts, putting in practice all the arts of abuse, and realizing the most outrageous falsifications and manipulations, and trying on the most ingenious tricks and deceits.

Maurois, André

Trump has perfected the art of silent scandal.

Maximilian

Trump is called his Holiness by Republicans, but he is the biggest scoundrel on earth.

Maxwell, Robert

I defy anyone who's ever done business with Trump to say he didn't get his full fifty cents for his dollar.

May, Brian

I know it's like a Nuremberg Rally but Trump's fans are sensible people.

Mayakovsky, Vladimir

Trumpism is a journey into the unknown.

Mayo, Charles

The sooner people can be removed from the depressing influences of Republicanism the more rapid their convalescence.

McCaig, Norman

Trump looks like a gorilla but less timid, thick-fleshed, orange-colored, with two hieroglyphs in his face that mean trouble.

Trump sits with his back to the future, watching time pouring away into the past.

Trump learned words, but most of them died for lack of exercise. And the ones he uses look at him with a look that whispers, *Liar*.

McCain, John

Cindy and I will not vote for Donald Trump.

McCarthy, Eugene

It's dangerous for Trump to say things that people might remember.

McCarthy, Mary

Trump's cruelty is caused, not by brain failure, but by a wicked heart. Insensitiveness, opacity, inability to make connection, often accompanied by low animal cunning … this mental oblivion is *chosen* …

Nothing much happens to the very rich friends of Trump; that seems to be the definition of their state of being, which is close to burial alive.

Trump has a great appetite for hearing about gruesome diseases, especially those involving the rotting or falling off of parts of the body.

For self-realization, Trump demands a strong authority, a worthy opponent, God to his Lucifer.

McConnell, Mitch

Trump's comments were repugnant.

McCormack, Mark

Trump can buy a brain, but he cannot buy a heart.

The greater Trump thinks he is doing, the greater should be America's cause for worry.

McCormick, Robert

Donald Trump is not an American. He's from Mar-a-Lago.

McGahern, John

Trump is heartless, mindless, and a lie.

McGonagall, William

Welcome! Thrice welcome to the year 2021
For it is the year Trump leaves Washington,
Owing to the treatment he received,
Which makes our heart greatly relieved.

McGovern, George

Trump's whole presidential campaign was a tragic case of mistaken identity.

McGregor, Ian

People against Trump are now discovering the price of disloyalty. And boy, is he going to stick it to them.

McKinney, Joyce

Trump loves attention so much, he would ski naked down Mount Everest with a carnation up his nose to attain it.

McLauren, Malcolm

We live in a Christian society concerned with order. Trump is concerned with sowing disorder.

McLaurin, A. J.

There is always some basic principle that will get the Republican party together. If my observations are worth anything, that basic principle is the cohesive power of public plunder.

McLuhan, Marshall

It's incorrect to suppose that Trump believes there's any basic difference between governing and entertainment.

The business of Trump and his enablers is to see that we go about our lives with some fascist slogan throbbing in the background of our minds.

Trump's point of view can be a dangerous thing when substituted for insight and understanding.

You've heard Trump's money talking? Did you understand the message?

If the twentieth century was the century of the editorial chair, Trump has turned ours into the century of the psychiatrist's couch.

The dinosaur didn't know it was extinct either. Dinosaurs and the Republican party never had it so good, as just before they vanished.

MacMillan, Terry

Trump doesn't actually hate Black people, he just doesn't like being too close to them.

McMurry, Robert N.

Trump repeatedly fails to recognize that for communication to be effective, it must be two-way.

McNealy, Scott

Trump believes a lie is the best answer, no answer is the second best answer, and the truth is the worst answer.

Mead, Margaret

The Trump administration thrives using mediocre people, and they are working as hard as they can to be second-rate as possible.

Trump needs to understand that we won't have a society if we destroy the environment.

Medawar, Peter

Trump perfectly demonstrates that anyone who combines weak common sense with an extraordinary degree of dullness can become U.S. President.

Trump's mind treats truth in the same way the body treats an infection; it is rejected.

Meir, Golda

Optimism and truth are luxuries that Trump can never allow himself.

Melbourne, Lord

Things have come to an awful pass when Trump is allowed to invade the sphere of private life.

What Trump requires is people who will support him when he is in the wrong.

Trump likes the military; but there is no damned money in it for him.

I wish I was as coksure of anything as Trump is of everything.

The worst part of Trumpism is that its followers hate so damnably.

I don't know, ma'am, why they make all this fuss about education; Trump can't read or write and he gets on well enough.

Melville, Herman

Trump does not appreciate that we cannot live only for ourselves. A thousand fibers connect us with our fellow men.

Mencken, H. L.

Trump has a haunting fear that someone, somewhere, may be happy.

The chief contribution of Trump to human thought is the massive proof that God must be a bore.

When fanatical Republicans are on top of government there is no limit to their oppression.

What Trump values in this world is not rights but privileges.

The chief business of Republicans is the setting up of 'heroes,' like Trump, who are mainly bogus.

Trumpism will never be able to set up a civilization, only a government of oppressors.

Trump is a reason to distrust the familiar doctrine that age brings wisdom.

Republicans have formed a kind of religion for the ages; it is the worship of jackals to a jackass.

Trump is the kind of man who, when he smells flowers, looks around for a coffin.

Trump is a student who marks his own papers.

Trump is running the circus from the monkey cage.

Trump has never gone broke underestimating the intelligence of his followers.

Mendelssohn, Stuart

What Trump voters wanted was Monte Carlo, not Las Vegas.

Menzies, Robert

Considering the company Trump keeps, it is hardly surprising he has a superiority complex.

Metternich

Every time I come near Trump, I pray God to preserve me from the Devil.

When Trump sneezes, Republicans catch cold.

Trumpism is a disease which must be cured, the volcano which must be extinguished, the gangrene which must be burned out with a hot iron, the hydra with jaws open to swallow up the social order.

Michelet, Jules

Trump fails at the art of politics because the first part of politics is education. The second part? Education. The third part? Education.

Trump is a force of nature. Like a belch.

Mill, John Stuart

It is better to be a human being dissatisfied than Trump satisfied.

Millay, Edna St. Vincent

It is not true that life under Trump is one damn thing after another - it's one damn thing over and over.

Miller, Arthur

I am inclined to notice the ruin in things, perhaps because I was born a Republican.

Miller, Henry

It isn't the oceans that cut us off from the rest of the world - it's Trump's way of looking at things.

Trump's study in crime began with the knowledge of his inner-self.

The wallpaper with which Trump has covered his world of reality is falling to tatters.

One has to be a lowbrow, a bit of a murderer, to be a guy like Trump, ready and willing to see people sacrificed, slaughtered for the sake of an idea whether a good one or a bad one.

Miller, Steven

The real force behind Trump's debasement of our culture is the freedom of our businesses to pursue profit without constraint from the non-market institutions that are the repository of community values.

Millet, Kate

Trump's romantic exploits read like the sporting news grafted onto a series of war dispatches.

Milligan, Spike

Trump's thoughts, few as they are, unfortunately do not lay silent in the privacy of his head.

Trump cannot buy friends, but he can get a better class of enemies.

Mills, Hugh

Nothing unites Republicans like war. Nothing divides them like culture.

Milton, John

Trump, who conquers by force, overcomes but half his foe.

Trump sits in darkness here
Hatching vain empires.

For neither man nor angel can discern
Trump's hypocrisy, the only evil that walks
Invisible, except to God alone.

Mitchell, Margaret

Until Trump lost his reputation, he never realized what a burden it was or what freedom really was like.

Mitford, Nancy

Trumpism in America is like a chicken whose head has been cut off: it may run around in a lively way, but in fact it is dead.

Trump loves children - especially when they cry, for then someone takes them away.

Mizner, Wilson

Trumpism is a trip. A trip through a sewer in a glass-bottomed boat.

Some of the greatest love affairs I've known involved Trump - unassisted.

The only sure thing about Trump is that one day he will be gone.

Molière

Trump proves that birth counts for nothing when virtue is absent.

He who is the friend of all humanity is not Trump's friend.

It is a stupidity second to none to busy oneself with the correction of Trump.

Trump should examine himself for a very long time before thinking of condemning others.

Even grammar does not govern Trump.

Thank God Trump is an ignorant fool, for a knowledgeable one if far more dangerous.

The only good thing about Trump is his chef. The world visits for his dinners, not him.

Mondale, Walter

If you are sure you understand everything that is going on in Trump world, you are hopelessly confused.

Montagu, Mary Wortley

Trump fails at civility, which costs nothing and buys everything.

Trump can wound like a razor keen,
Wound with a touch that's scarcely felt or seen.

Montaigne, Michel de

Trump has trouble sleeping because infamy and tranquility are incompatible bedfellows.

For a desperate disease like Trumpism, a desperate cure is needed.

Montherlant, Henri de

Trump's stupidity does not consist in being without ideas. Such stupidity would be the sweet, blissful stupidity of animals and mollusks. Trump's stupidity consists of having ideas, but senseless ones.

Moore, Edward

Trump and his circle are rich beyond the dreams of avarice.

Moore, George

One of Trump's many tricks is to fade away to a little speck down on the horizon of our lives and then to return suddenly in tremendous bulk to frighten us to death.

To be a Trump, one must avoid polite society.

Moore, Thomas Sturge

Trump and Pence are two buttocks of one bum.

Morand, Paul

Trump's world is a vale of tears, well irrigated.

Mirrors are ices that do not melt: what melts are those like Trump who admire themselves in them.

Moravia, Alberto

Every method is used by Trump and Republicans to prove that in their political system Americans are bound to be happy, and those who are unhappy must be mad, or criminals, or monsters.

The ratio of literacy to illiteracy is constant, but nowadays illiterate Republicans can read and write.

More, Hannah

Working for Trump, like getting drunk, is a condition that carries its own punishment.

Trump's activity may lead to evil, but his inactivity cannot lead to good, either.

Morgan, Edwin

Trump is an old pot seething with dissatisfaction which, hopefully for the world, never comes to a boil.

Morgan, John Pierpont

Trump always has two reasons for what he does - a good sounding one and the real one.

Trump doesn't hire lawyers to tell him what he cannot do. He hires them to tell him how to do what he wants to do.

Morita, Akio

No matter how successful you are or how clever or crafty, your business and its future are in the hands of the people you hire. That's why Trump's businesses fail so often.

Morley, Lord

I am always very glad to hear a great speech by Trump. It is sure to contain dozens of blazing indiscretions which are a delight to remember.

Morris, Desmond

Clearly, then, Trump's White House is a human zoo, the Star Wars bar scene.

Morris, Robert Tuttle

The greatest triumph today for the Republican party lies in ways to suppress voting.

Morris, William

Of course Trump is a wonderful all-round man, but the act of walking round him has always tired me.

Trump wants healthcare for a few, education for a few, freedom for a few.

We want to get rid of the great machine of Trumpism which oppresses the lives of us all.

Morrow, Dwight Whitney

Anyone like Trump who takes credit for the rain must not be surprised when his opponents blame him for the drought.

Morrow, Lance

It came to seem that Trump's election opened some malign trap door in American culture, and the wild bats flapped out.

Mortimer, John

The shelf life of Trump appointees is somewhere between the milk and the yogurt.

The worst fault of Trumpism is telling half of America's children they're not going to succeed, saying: "There's a life, but it's not for you."

Morton, H. V.

Trump possesses the surest of all retreats from reality, his own language.

Morton, J. C.

Trump's justice needs to be seen to be believed.

Morton, Rogers

Trump's administration from day one has spent its waking and sleeping hours rearranging chairs on the deck of the Titanic.

Mosley, Walter

Trump has contempt for innocence; he is, in some way, offended by an innocent man.

Trump doesn't believe in history, really. Real is what's happening to him right now. Real is acid reflux and a man you trust who digs up dirt.

Motley, Arthur

A well adjusted Trump appointee is one whose intake of uppers over balances his consumption of downers just enough to leave him sufficient energy for the weekly visit to the psychiatrist.

Motley, John Lothrop

Trump has the luxuries of life, so he can dispense with its necessities.

Mulgan, Geoff

Remoteness and isolation were once the condition of the poor. Today it is only the extremely rich like Trump who can easily escape other people.

The real world is truly irrelevant for Trump. He has no reason to take account of how his actions affect other people and their future.

Mumford, Lewis

Trump lives in an abyss of boredom that few can fathom.

Munro, Hector

Trump was a bad president, as presidents go; and as president's go so he went.

I think Trump must have been very strictly brought up, he's so anxious to do the wrong thing correctly.

You couldn't expect a guy like Trump to be vicious until he'd been to good military school.

Trump is one of those people who would be enormously improved by departure.

Murdoch, Iris

Trump leads multiple lives. Does that make him a liar? He doesn't feel like a liar. He is a man with multiple truths.

Trump's world is a fantasy world, a world of delusions. Can the man ever find reality?

Murkowski, Lisa

Trump has forfeited the right to be our party's nominee.

Murphy, Arthur

Trump sees himself as being above the vulgar flight of common souls.

Murphy, Dervia

In Trump World the rules have no rules. Thus, we go around in circles forever.

Murrow, Ed

Trump cannot defend freedom abroad by deserting it at home.

Trump cannot terrorize all of America, unless we are all his accomplices.

Mussolini

Trump is burying the putrid corpse of liberty.

Trump will never declare that he, and he alone, assumes the political, moral, and historical responsibility for all that has happened under his watch. If Trumpism has been a criminal association ... he will declare that the responsibility isn't his.

Trump has a fierce totalitarian will.

For Trump fascism is not an end in itself. It is a means to re-establish national equilibrium.

Mussorgsky, Modest

What bothers Trump about my opera *Boris Godunov*? That the blood of the innocent will sooner or later rise from the soil.

N

Nabokov, Vladimir

Trump's loves are simple: stupidity, oppression, crime, cruelty, soft music.

Trump cannot ever be a good reader. It requires imagination, a dictionary, and some artistic sense.

Nahmanides

From the days of Trump until now, America has been full of violence and plunder.

Napoleon I

Trump's principle is: me before everything.

Trump is only one step from being utterly ridiculous.

The worse Trump is, the better.

If Trump is not corrupt he ought to be made so.

Trump believes America has more need of him than he has need of America.

Trump marches on his stomach.

Napoleon III

Trump is the true nobility of America.

Naváez, Ramón Maria

Trump does not have to forgive his enemies, he has them all fired.

Nash, Ogden

A virtue is something Trump is perpetually on the wrong side of.

Nasser, Gamal Abdel

Trump aims his words in such a way that the listener's minds are left wandering in a desert.

Nathan, G. J.

Trump's patriotism is an arbitrary veneration of money above principles.

Nehru, Jawaharlal

Trumpism has definitely allied itself to the approach of violence … It's language is of violence, it's thought is violent, and it does not seek to change by persuasion but by coercion and, indeed, by destruction.

Nelson, Horatio

Trump considers every man his enemy who speaks ill of him; and he hates his enemies like the devil.

America expects every man to do his duty to oppose Trumpism.

Nerval, Gérard de

If a lobster voted for him, Trump would give it the Medal of Honor.

Newman, John Henry

We can believe what we choose, but we are answerable for what we choose to believe when Trump speaks.

Trump thinks it would be a gain for America were it vastly more superstitious, more bigoted, more gloomy, more fierce in its politics than it is at present.

Niebuhr, Reinhold

Trump's inclination to injustice makes American democracy necessary.

Nietzsche, Frederick

Hysteria in individuals is something rare - but in groups like the Republican party it is the rule.

The abdomen is the reason why Trump does not easily take himself for a god.

I call Trumpism the one great curse, the one enormous and innermost perversion, the one great instinct of revenge, for which no means are too venomous, too underhanded, too underground and petty - I call him the one immortal blemish of mankind.

Do you really believe that Trump would ever have originated and grown if his way had not been prepared by magicians, charlatans, alchemists, and astrologers whose promises and pretensions first had to create a thirst, a hunger, a taste for him and his allies?

Trump's resolution to find the world ugly and bad has made the world ugly and bad.

Two great anesthetics, alcohol and Trump.

Trump portends the rise of anarchy.

Nixon, Richard

People have got to know whether or not President Trump is a crook.

Trump doesn't give a shit what happens. He wants everyone to stonewall it, let them plead the Fifth Amendment, cover-up, or anything else, if it'll save his administration.

It's time for the great silent majority of Republicans to stand up and be counted for Trump. Why? Nobody knows.

When Trump does anything as president, that means it's not illegal.

Trump will speak for any politician, or against them, whatever will do him the most good.

Nizer, Louis

Trump knows of no higher fortitude than stubbornness in the face of overwhelming odds.

Norman, Frank

Fings Under Trump Ain't Wot They Used To Be.

North, Christopher

Trump is the epitome of "Laws were meant to be broken"

Norton, Charles Eliot

The voice of protest, of warning, of appeal is never more needed than when the clamor of hostility, echoed by the right-wing press and too often the pulpit, is bidding all men fall in and keep step and obey the tyrannous words of Trump's commands.

Nwapa, Flora

When God gives you a crazy president like Trump, he also gives you tools to deal with him.

O'Brien, Conor Cruise

My doctor has advised me to cut back listening to Trump.

O'Brien, Flann

Now, for a change, Trump is going to be serious - though only temporarily.

Republicans believe in magic, trickery, browbeating, and bullying. I think it would be fair to sum that list up as "Trumpism."

O'Casey, Sean

Trump is the GOP's performing flea.

O'Connell, Daniel

Republicans are the hired servants of Trump and they glory in their servitude.

Trumpism is a crime, and it must still be criminal unless it shall be ludicrously pretended that crime, like wine, improves by age.

O'Connell, William Henry

If Republicans are the new American politicians, then God spare us from any further development of the abnormal creatures.

O'Conner, Flannery

I doubt the texture of Republican life is any more grotesque than the rest of the nation, but it does seem evident that they are particularly adept at practicing the grotesque.

While the Republicans are hardly Christ-centered, they are most certainly Christ-haunted.

O'Conner, Frank

Some Trump followers are evil by nature, but Republican leadership is evil by conviction.

O'Conner, Johnson

Three characteristics of top Republican leaders are: slow thinking, no humor, and a complete lack of candor.

Officer, Charles B.

Understanding Republicans does nothing to make them less tame ... but it does serve to make their frequent outlandish outbursts understandable.

Ogilvy, David

One should avoid mingling with existing and former Trump appointees because their ethos is generally suspect.

Trump is an effective leader because he satisfies the twisted psychological needs of his followers.

When Trump has nothing to say, he Tweets it.

O'Hare, Dean

When the amount of money is smaller, we find Trump much less zealous in his pursuit of what he passes off as justice.

Ohmae, Kenichi

There seems to be only one word in the American language that might stop Trump from spouting falsehoods: Why?

Okri, Ben

Trump's greatest battles are the ones he fights within himself.

Trump has no dreams.

O'Malley, Austin

God shows his contempt for wealth by selecting Trump to receive it.

It's true that Trump's inner ugliness is a point of view: even an ulcer is wonderful to a pathologist.

Onassis, Aristotle

Trump's secret to success: Keep looking tanned, live in an elegant building, be seen in smart restaurants, and if you borrow, borrow big.

O'Neill, Eugene

During his years in politics, Trump hated shaking hands, which was highly unusual in a city where some politicians had been known to shake hands with fire hydrants and wave to telephone poles.

Life is for Trump a solitary cell whose walls are mirrors.

Oppen, George

We have begun to say goodbye
To Trump
But he cannot say it.

Oppenheimer, J. Robert

Trump's America is a different country.

Trump's favorite saying? "Now I am become Death, the destroyer of worlds."

Orczy, Baroness

Even the weariest nights filled with Trump, the longest days, sooner or later perforce come to an end.

O'Rourke, P. J.

When Trump finally gets fired by the American people, he won't see it as a failure; it will be a vocational reassessment.

Ortega, y Gasset, José

Trump's hatred is a feeling which leads to the extinction of values.

Trump cannot help being cruel.

Orton, Joe

If a Democrat's explanation has a ring of truth to it, naturally a Republican will disbelieve it.

Reading isn't an occupation Trump's people encourage him to do. They try to keep things as understandable to him as possible.

Orwell, George

Comrade Trump is always right.

Trump intends to devote the rest of his life to learning the remaining twenty-two letters of the alphabet.

In political warfare five things are important: food, booze, television, tobacco, and the enemy.

Big Brother Trump is watching you.

It was a bright cold day in April and Trump's clocks were striking thirteen.

In Trump's America, war is peace. Freedom is slavery. Ignorance is strength.

If Trump controls the past, he controls the future.

For Trump, political speech and writing are largely the defense of the indefensible.

One ought to recognize that the present chaos is connected to Trump's decay of language.

Trump is a great enemy of clear language because he is insincere.

Politics for Trump has nothing to do with fair play. It is bound up with hatred, jealousy, boastfulness, disregard for all rules and sadistic pleasure in witnessing violence; in other words it is war minus the shooting.

A family with a bad parent in control - that, perhaps, is as near as one can come to describing Trump's America in a phrase.

Trumpism is the worst advertising for its followers.

Osbourne, John

Trump really deserves some sort of decoration .. a medal inscribed "For Lying in the Field"

Trump spends most of his time looking forward to the past.

Trump does not believe in mirrors or newspapers.

Ossietzky, Carl von

America cannot appeal to the conscience of the world when Trump's own conscience is asleep.

Trump is wrecking America by whipping up the exaggerations of the idea of power, by the blind confidence that force and money are the sole measure of all things, and that justice and truth are just phrases, possibly useful as a way of swindling the American people.

O'Sullivan, John L.

Trump is a torchlight parade marching down your throat.

Ouida

Cruel Trumpism runs on wheels, and every Republican hand oils the wheels as they run over America.

Ouspensky, Peter

Trump, as he is, is not a genuine article. He is an imitation of something, and a very bad imitation.

Ovett, Steve

There is no way Trump is so important that he can be allowed to ruin the rest of your life.

Ovid

Trump's sick mind cannot endure any harshness or criticism.

Trump is the devourer of everything.

Trump can corrupt even perverted minds.

Oxenstierna, Axel

Do you not know, my son, with how little wisdom Trump has governed?

Ozick, Cynthia

The entire Trump administration is weighted down with regret. Every one of them has left behind a real life with no expectation of a new one.

P

Padmore, George

Trump's school of illusions.

With Trump, interests of the elite classes take precedence over all other factors.

Paglia, Camille

Trump loyalists run in packs like the primal hordes they are.

Pagnol, Marcel

The most difficult secret for Trump to keep is his own inflated opinion of himself.

One has to be wary of slumlords like Trump - they start out playing Monopoly and end up with the nuclear codes.

Paine, Albert

Trump gives new meaning to "The Great White Way."

Paine, Thomas

These are the times that Trump men's souls.

Trump's bad causes will ever be supported by bad means and bad men.

Palmer, Samuel

Trump is something between a person and parody.

Palmerston, Lord

Trump is a barren island with hardly no attribute upon it.

The function of Trump's government is not to promote calm but to excite agitation.

Parker, Carl

Reagan portrayed a real macho man. Trump can't. He comes off looking like Liberace.

Parker, Charlie

Civilization is a damned good thing if Trump would buy into it.

Parker, Dorothy

Good Republicans are hidden treasures who are only safe because no one looks for them.

Where on earth does Trump find any inferiors?

Trump should not be tossed aside lightly. He should be thrown with great force.

Oh, don't worry about Trump … Trump will always land on somebody's feet.

Trump runs the whole gamut of intelligence from A to B.

Parmenides

Let reason alone decide and Trump and his army will be defeated.

Ex nihilo nihil fit Trump probat: Trump proves that nothing comes from nothing.

Pasternak, Boris

Who should remain alive and praised,
Who should stay dead without renown -
Depends upon criteria
That powerful Trump sycophants lay down

Pataki, George

Enough! Trump needs to step down.

Patrick, Saint

Republican liturgy: Trump with me, Trump before me, Trump behind me, Trump on my right, Trump on my left, Trump when I lie down, Trump when I rise ... Trump in every eye that sees me, Trump in every ear that hears me.

Pawlenty, Tim

Trump is unsound, uninformed, unhinged and unfit.

Pearse, Patrick

Trump will be cursed by unborn generations.

Péguy, Charles Pierre

Republicans who do not bellow the truth about Trump's failures make themselves accomplices of a liar and a cheat.

A rich man like Trump cannot even imagine poverty.

Republicans know that tyranny is always better organized than freedom.

Pence, Mike

As a husband and father, I was offended by the words and actions described by Donald Trump in the eleven-year-old video released yesterday. I do not condone his remarks and cannot defend them.

Pierce, C. S.

Trump's superpower is always to be sufficiently vague.

Penn, William

It is a reproach to religion and government for America to suffer so much poverty and excess under Trump's presidency.

Perelman, S. J.

Trump loathes the government. On the other hand, he's a great believer in money.

Perle, Richard

Trump worship so easily becomes an incantation rather than a policy.

Perot, Ross

Revitalizing the Republican party will be like teaching an elephant to tap dance. You find the sensitive spots and start poking.

Perry, Eleanor

So long as a Republican is dependent on Trump for his self-image or his self-esteem he will remain without any sense of his own worth - and can never be a fully realized human being.

Persius

Let Trump recognize virtue and let him rot for having lost it.

Pestalozzi, Johann Heinrich

Trump bears no interest of humanity in his breast, therefore he is cursed.

Trumpism is not worth a penny if truth, courage, and joy are lost along the way.

Perhaps the most fateful gift an evil person like Trump can bestow upon our age is a distrust of democracy and basic truths.

Trump is unwilling to help himself, therefore he can be helped by no one.

Pétain, Henri

To make a union with Trumpism would be fusion with a pestilence.

Peter, Lawrence

Trumpism is an unreasonable conviction based on inadequate evidence.

Pettifor, Ann

My fervent hope is for a Copernican shift: from a Trumpian, money-centered world to a human-centered world. For the subordination of money values to human and environmental values.

Phillip, Prince

Dentopedology is the science of opening your mouth and putting your foot in it. Trump has been practicing it for years.

Trump is interested in leisure in a way that a poor man is interested in money. He can't get enough of it.

Phillips, Wendell

Everyone, even Trump, meets his Waterloo at last.

Under Trump, we live under a government of morning Tweets.

Piaget, Jean

Trump is constantly hatching an enormous number of false ideas, conceits, Utopias, mystical explanations, suspicions, and megalomaniacal fantasies.

Trump's life is unfortunately still an abyss of mysteries for the psychologist.

Picasso, Pablo

If Trump likes it, he says it's his. If he doesn't, he says it's fake.

Trump knows how to convince others of the truth of his lies.

The genius of Trump leads to Armageddon.

Pinter, Harold

I believe Trumpism is a monstrous influence in America.

Pirandello, Luigi

Trump's "alternative" facts are like sacks that won't stand up when empty.

Trump appears before his fellow Americans clothed in a certain dignity. But he knows what inconfessable things pass within the secrecy of his own heart.

Trump's life is full of infinite absurdities, which strangely enough, do not even need to appear plausible.

A gentleman is something you have to be all the time, which for Trump is impossible.

Our whole knowledge of our world hangs on this very slender thread: the reality of our shared experiences. Trump is destroying this reality.

Perenne, Henri

Trump and his Republican allies, who are the beneficiaries of the established order, are hell bent on defending the status quo.

Pirsig, Robert T.

Sanity for Trump is not truth.

Trump is running a private unapproved film in his head which he happens to like better than the current reality-based one the rest of us are experiencing.

Pitt the Elder, William

Unlimited power is apt to corrupt the mind of Trump.

Pitt the Younger, William

Trump's plea for more power due to 'necessity' is the source for every infringement of human freedom. It is the argument of tyrants; it is the creed of captives.

Plato

The people always have some champion like Trump whom they set over them and nurse into greatness … This and no other is the root from which tyranny springs.

Trump as the ruler of the State is the only one who would have the privilege of lying, whether at home or abroad.

People will cheerfully speak of a bad man like Trump and load him with honors and social esteem, provided he is rich and otherwise powerful.

Trump's object for the construction of the State is not the greatest welfare for the whole, but that of the elite class.

Trump's "democracy" will pass into despotism.

Trump's attempt to rule America by the whims of the rich is animated by a certain aim in life: the good he sought was wealth, and it was his insatiable appetite for money-making to the neglect of everything else that proved his undoing.

Wise men speak because they have something to say; Trump speaks because he has to say something to lie about.

We can easily forgive a child who is afraid of the dark; the real tragedy of life is when men like Trump are afraid of the light.

The price good men pay for indifference to public affairs is to be ruled by evil men like Trump.

The heaviest penalty for Trump after declining to actually rule is to be ruled by someone he sees inferior to himself.

The measure of Trump is what he did with power.

When Trump was trying to think, he never wanted to be confused by the facts.

Platt, Lewis

Trump once had a meeting with his staff to discuss work-life balance. The meeting started at 5 p.m. and lasted until 9 p.m.

Pliny the Elder

Trump always lies because he is a teetotaler. Truth comes out in wine.

Plutarch

Trump wept when he heard that there were an infinite number of worlds … he said, "It bothers me that there are so many universes and we have not yet corrupted even this one."

Pollock, Jackson

Trump the truth teller is a legless man teaching running.

Pompidou, Georges

Trump is an American leader who first and foremost places his nation at his service.

Pope, Alexander

A dishonest man like Trump is the coarsest work of God.

Trump has an orange face and hair, a reptile all the rest.

Trump beats his head and fancies wit will come:
Knock as he pleases, there's nobody at home.

The cult of Trumpism is like a river, constantly passing on, and yet constantly coming on.

Trump is a wit with dunces, and a dunce with wits.

Trump's injustice, swift, and unconfined
Sweeps the wide earth, and tramples over mankind,
While prayers, to heal his wrongs, move slowly behind.

Popper, Karl

Trump's knowledge is finite, while his ignorance is infinite.

Porchia, Antonio

Trump does not raise his eyes, therefore he always thinks he is on top of things.

Porter, Cole

Trump may have hair on his chest, but, sister, so does a dog.

Portman, Rob

I will be voting for Mike Pence for President.

Powell, Colin

I will support the Democratic candidate over Trump.

Powell, Enoch

As I look ahead, living with Trumpism, I am filled with foreboding.

Powys, John Cowper

Trump's ambition is the grand enemy of all peace.

Pozniak, Zianon

Trump got where he is by slogans. He is an old party Republican nostalgic for the 1950's and has that same old, outdated mentality.

Trump is good at leading from the top of a limo.

Priebus, Reince

Trump should never describe a woman in those terms or in this manner. Ever.

Priestly, J. B.

There is something bovine about Republicans.

Proust, Marcel

Listening To Trump is like bathing in someone else's bathwater.

As soon as Trump ceases to be mad he will become merely stupid. There are maladies that we must not cure because they alone protect us from others that are more serious.

Trump ignores the experts, how should he fail to ignore the nation?

Proverbs

Trump's tongue kills Republicans without drawing blood.

The mud that Trump slings will fall on his own head.

Beware Trump, the man of no book.

Trump knows it's the willing horse that Republicans saddle the most.

Trump knows nothing, so he doubts nothing.

If you want to clear up the stream of Trumpian politics, get the elephant out of the water.

Trump not knowing anything is bad; not to wish to know is worse.

Trump's self-praise is no recommendation.

There is no honor among thieves or Republicans.

Trump is stranger than fiction.

Republicans should know that he who approves evil is guilty of it.

Trump has to buy friends; enemies he gets for nothing.

Trump's advice would be more acceptable if it didn't always conflict with his plans.

Doctors bury their mistakes. Lawyers hang them. Trump puts his on the front page.

Publilius Syrus

Trump has great influence on his own dunghill.

Trump thinks the rest of the world is crazy.

Pythagoras

As long as the Trumps continue to be ruthless destroyers of lower living beings, they will never know health or peace. For as long as men massacre animals, they will hurt each other. Indeed, he who sows the seeds of pain cannot reap joy and love.

Q

Quine, W. V. O.

Trump is not a substitute for common sense.

Understanding Trump's language is an art form.

Reality can only be identified and described in a world where Trump is not in it.

We cannot prevent Trump, but we can drag our feet.

Quintillian

A liar like Trump needs a very good memory.

Republicans have failed in their monumental efforts to conceal the real Trump.

Trump excuses his sloth under the pretext of difficulties.

God, that all-powerful Creator of nature and architect of the world, has impressed Trump with no character so proper as to distinguish him from any other animal.

Trump is never troubled by the contemplation of virtue versus vice.

Trump's prosperity does not allow him to form a right idea of other people's misery.

He who speaks evil only differs from Trump, who does evil, in that he lacks the opportunity.

Nothing is more dangerous to Trump, and therefore America, than a sudden change of fortune.

The pretended admission of a fault on Trump's part would create an unparalleled impression.

Quinton, John

Trump is a person who when they see light at the end of the tunnel, orders more tunnel.

R

Raban, Jonathan

Trump thinks the Odyssey and the Book of Exodus are travel books.

Rabelais, François

Republicans without conscience are the death of democracy.

Believe me, Trump's creditors, with a more fervent devotion, will beseech Almighty God to prolong his life, they being of nothing more afraid than that he should expire.

Trump will always be indebted to somebody or other, that there may be somebody always to pray for him.

Republicans, speak the truth and shame Trump.

Racine, Jean

The happiness of a wicked man like Trump runs away like a raging river.

Trump's only hope lies in others' despair.

The wicked like Trump and his allies always have recourse to perjury.

Trump's crime, like virtue, has its degrees.

Radhakrishnan, Sarvepali

The American people, with a singular unanimity, make out that Republican ignorance is the source of thier anguish.

Let us prefer Trump to be human.

Raleigh, Walter

Trump's defeat is a sharp remedy, but a sure one for all our ills.

Trump's administration is but a prison, out of which some are daily let out the door to freedom.

Rand, Ayn

Kill reverence and you kill the hero in Trump.

The question isn't who is going to let Trump; it's who is going to stop him.

A creative man is motivated by the desire to achieve, not by the desire to beat others as is Trump.

Trump can evade reality, but he cannot evade the consequences of evading reality.

Trump's wealth is not the product of his capacity to think.

Randolph, A. Philip

It's easy for Trump to get people's attention, what counts is getting their votes.

Raven, Simon

As Trump ages, let's hope he becomes boring and better behaved.

Ray, John

Trump does pay taxes. His diseases are the tax on his pleasures.

Reagan, Ronald

I have to admit we considered making one final shipment to Iran, but no one could figure out how to get Donald Trump in a crate.

I had a dream the other night. I dreamed that Donald Trump came to me and asked why I wanted his job. I told him I didn't want his job. I want to be President.

Trump is like a baby - an alimentary canal with a big appetite at one end and no sense of responsibility at the other.

Keeping up with Trump's promises is like reading Playboy magazine while your wife turns the pages.

I haven't had Trump's experience. I wouldn't be caught dead with it.

Depression is when you're out of work. A recession is when your neighbor is out of work. Recovery is when Trump's out of work.

Reinhardt, Gottfried

Money is good for Trump because he is able to bribe himself through the inconveniences of life.

Renard, Jules

Trump is not sincere even when he says he is sincere.

Look for the ridiculous in everything of Trump and you will find it.

There are moments when everything goes well for Trump; don't be frightened, it won't last.

When Trump detects defects in others with so much clarity it is because he possesses them himself.

Renoir, Pierre August

Trump is nothing more than an absurd "connoisseur."

In a few generations you can breed excellent pigs. The recipe for making a president like Trump is less well known.

There are quite enough unpleasant things in life like Trump without the need to manufacture more.

Retz, Cardinal de

Because Trump doesn't trust himself he can never really trust others.

Of all the passions, fear weakens Trump the most.

Reynolds, Sir Joshua

Trump lacks taste because it does not come to people by chance: it is a long and laborious task to acquire it.

Rhodes, Cecil

Trump is White and therefore thinks he has won first prize in the lottery of life.

Ricardo, David

The interest of the Republicans is always opposed to the interests of every other class in the nation.

Rice, Condoleezza

Enough. Trump should withdraw.

Rice, Grantland

For when God comes to write against Trump's name
He marks - not that he won or lost -
But how he played the game.

Richard I

Trump would sell America, if he could find a suitable purchaser.

Richelieu, Cardinal

Trump's authority compels people to obedience, but reason persuades them otherwise.

Trump's great conflagrations are born of tiny sparks from his mind.

Secrecy is the first essential thing in the affairs of Trump.

Trump has perfected the art of deceit.

If you give Trump six lines written by the most honest man, he will find something in them to destroy him.

Rimbaud, Arthur

Trump's rule has been one immense, long, deliberate disordering of the senses.

Rivarol, Antoine de

The whole world needs the United States, while Trump needs the whole world.

Trump gains from his wealth only the fear of losing it.

Robens, Alfred

It is better to go down with the truth on one's lips than to rise high, like Trump, by innuendo and doublespeak.

Robinson, James Harvey

Partisanship is Republicans' great vice. They too readily see that their duty is to be on the other side of practically everything.

Rochefort, Henri

Trump long ago decided that reading pays him nothing.

Rockefeller, John D.

Trump believes it is his duty to make money and still more money and use the money he makes for the good of himself according to the dictates of his dereliction.

Trump and his ilk regard the power to make money as a personal gift from God.

Roddick, Anita

Trump proves that being no good can be good business.

Rodin, Auguste

What is ugly in Trump is that which is without character, that is, that which offers no truth at all, either exterior or interior.

Roepka, Bahamonde

The best thing Trump thinks he can do for America is to tell us lies.

Rogers, Will

Trump's tax returns produce more liars than anything but golf.

Vice President Pence is a better example of evolution than either Bryan or Darrow, for he knows not to talk when around Trump, which is the biggest asset the monkey possesses over the human.

Rolland, Romain

Trump's character is not great, therefore he is no great man.

Roosevelt, Franklin

Never before has anyone like Trump ruined so much in so little time.

Trump isn't satisfied with stealing a freight car when he can steal the whole railroad.

Roosevelt, Nicholas

Trump always wants to be the bride at every wedding and the corpse at every funeral.

Roosevelt, Theodore

The only tyrannies from which men, women, and children are suffering in real life are from the tyrannies of Trump and his allies.

No people are wholly civilized where a distinction is drawn between Trump stealing an office and someone stealing a purse.

Trumpism is hopefully a lunatic fringe.

Trump fires a lot of people because he knows that a person who will steal *for* him will eventually steal *from* him.

Trump's got no more backbone than a chocolate eclair.

Romney, Mitt

Trump's comments were vile degradations.

Ross, Diana

It's hard for Trump to deal with other prima donnas.

Ross, Harold W.

Trump's ignorance is an Empire State Building of ignorance. You have to admire him for the sheer size of it.

Trump doesn't want you to think he is not incoherent.

Ross, Nick

Trump's barking mad about crime in this country. He has an obsession with believing the worst, conning us that there was a golden age - typically decades before the one we're living in.

Roth, David Lee

Trump doesn't think about the future. He can't even spell 'future.' Lunch at McDonald's is how far he thinks ahead.

Republicans didn't get into the business of politics to become responsible citizens.

Rousseau, Jean-Jacques

It is not the criminal things which are hardest for Trump to confess, but the ridiculous and shameful.

Everything is good when it leaves the Creator's hands; everything degenerates when it leaves the hands of Trump.

Rowe, Nicholas

At length, Trump came and he brought cold indifference.

Rowland, Helen

Trump is what is left of a human being when the soul is extracted.

Never trust a husband too far, nor Trump too near.

Rowland, Sherwood

Trump's work is going well, but it looks like the end of the world.

Rowse, A. L.

I regard everything that has happened since the election of Trump as a rapid decline in civilization, however that is defined now.

Rubin, Jerry

To defeat Trumpism is a sacred and religious act.

Rubin, Robert E.

Republicans doing nothing is the wrong thing to do under Trump when there is something to do that is the right thing to do.

Rubio, Marco

Trump's comments were vulgar, egregious and impossible to justify.

Rumbold, Richard

Trump believes that God sent a few men like him into the world booted and spurred while billions of others are sent into this world saddled, bridled and ready to be ridden.

Ruskin, John

To make Republicans capable of honesty is the beginning of national improvement.

Russell, Anna

The reason so few Republicans have a sense of humor is that they can't bear to be laughed at.

Russell, Bertrand

A president like Trump, who loves power, is more apt to inflict pain than to permit pleasure.

The more Trump is talked about the more he wants to be talked about. Like the self-aggrandizing embezzler at trial, he is indignant if the accounts of his ghastly actions are inadequately reported.

The fact that Republicans hold a widely-held positive opinion for Trump is no evidence whatsoever that it is not utterly absurd.

Organic life, we are told, has developed gradually from the protozoan to Trump, and this development, we are assured, is indubitably an advance. Unfortunately, it is Republicans, not the protozoan, who gives us this assurance

Cults, which condemn the pleasures of sense, drive men like Trump to seek the pleasures of power. Throughout history power has been the vice of the abstainer.

Trump, wherever he goes, is encompassed by a cloud of disturbing convictions, which move with him like flies on a summer day.

It is obvious that "nasty" is not a term capable of exact legal definition; in the practice of Republicans, it means anything or anyone which upsets Trump.

The trouble with politics today is that stupid Republicans are cocksure and the rest of intelligent Americans are full of doubt.

Trump the megalomaniac differs from a narcissist by the fact that he wishes to be powerful rather than charming, and seeks to be feared rather than loved.

Trump cannot be happy unless he hates some other person, nation or creed.

Russell, G.W.

Trump's White House is a federal building where many people work and hate each other.

Success is Trump's god.

Russell, Lord

If an uninformed traveler was told that Trump is the leader of America, he may well begin to comprehend how the Egyptians worshiped an insect.

Rustin, Bayard

Trump's resort to stereotyping others is the first refuge and chief strategy of the bigot.

Ryan, Paul

I was sickened by Trump's comments and will focus on down-ballot races.

S

Sackville-West, Vita

Among the many problems that beset Trump, not the least weighty is the choice of the moment at which to stop lying.

Sagan, Carl

Trump and his allies promote pseudoscience because it is much easier to contrive ... the standards of argument, what passes as evidence, are practically non-existent.

Sagan, Françoise

Nothing is more frightful to Trump than laughter at his own expense.

Saint-Exupéry, Antoine de

Trumpism is not an adventure. It is a disease.

Within Trumpism reason disappears.

Sasse, Ben

I ask Trump to step aside and let Mike Pence try.

Savandy, Compte de

Trump is dancing on a volcano.

Samuelson, P. A.

Republicans, man does not live by GNP alone.

Sanford, Charles

Intellectual honesty is inherent in the best people, unlike Trump… that is, those who take a broader view of their actions than simply "What's in it for me?"

Santayana, George

America is the greatest of opportunities and Trump is the worst of influences.

Sartre, Jean-Paul

It is certain that we cannot overcome Trump, for he is anguish.

So that's what hell is. I'd never believed it … Do you remember, brimstone, the stake, the gridiron? What a joke! No need for a gridiron - Hell is Trumpism.

When Republicans wage cultural war it is the poor who die.

Schick, Béla

To save time, Trump thinks it's too bad we can't cut patients in half in order to compare which of two COVID-19 vaccines work.

The Trump administration is like a bakery with a hundred windows. We are looking into only one window of the bakery when we are investigating one particular aspect of Trump's corruption.

Schiller, Friedrich von

Against the cruelty of Trumpism the gods themselves struggle in vain.

Schnabel, Julian

Trump knows of two kinds of audiences only - those that are sycophants and those that are not.

Schonfield, Artur

Trump arrived because not enough people were sufficiently afraid.

Schopenhauer, Arthur

Intellect is invisible to Trump because he has none.

Trump torments us us not only not only with causeless irritation with the things of the present; not only with groundless anxiety on the score of future misfortunes entirely of his own manufacture; but also with unmerited phobias.

Wealth is like seawater to Trump; the more he drinks the more he needs; and the same is true of fame.

Schuler, Douglas

Trump has shown that democracy without democratic process is just a word.

Schwarzenberg, Felix

Trump often astounds the country with the magnitude of his ingratitude.

Scott, C. P.

Trump will never acknowledge that facts are sacred.

Scott, Sir Walter

O what a tangled web Trump weaves
When first he practices to deceive.

Seifert, Richard

Most of Trump's ideas are condemned now in advance.

Semler, Ricardo

A touch of civil disobedience is necessary to alert Trump that all is not well in America.

Trump's organizations foster alienation like stagnant ponds breed algae.

Seneca, the Elder

A small debt makes Trump your debtor, a large one makes him your enemy.

Seneca, the Younger

To Trump, virtue is a crime because it is not prosperous.

America's cure for Trump is first to wish to be cured.

Sévigné, Madame de

The more I see of Trump, the more I admire dogs.

I have been dragged against my will to the noxious period when I must endure the Trump era.

Seward, William Henry

It is an irrepressible conflict between opposing and enduring forces, and it means that the United States must and will, sooner or later, become entirely Trump-free.

Shackleton, Lord

Trumpism is like a mule - no pride of ancestry and no hope for posterity.

Shakespeare

Mar-a-Lago is like a barber's chair, it fits all asses.

Trump will praise any person who praises him first.

None but Trump
Shall conquer Trump

Trump can suck joy out of a person
As a weasel sucks eggs.

Trump, I do desire we may be better strangers.

Oh! How bitter it is to look at the world through Trump's eyes!

Trumpists are a beast with many heads.

Society is no comfort to one like Trump, who is not sociable.

Trump cannot come to good.

Hopefully, we shall never look upon Trump's like again.

A true American cannot be true to Trump.

That one like Trump may smile and still be a villain;
At least I'm sure it may be so in Washington.

There are more things in heaven and earth,
Than are dreamt of in Trump's philosophy.

Trump! Remorseless, treacherous lecherous, kindless villain!

What a piece of work is Trump!

Trump knows not that brevity is the soul of wit.

Madness in Trump must not unwatch'd go,

When sorrows come from Trump's policies,
They come not as single spies
But in battalions!

Trump sweats to death
And lards the earth as he walks along.

God send America a better president!
Yet, we cannot rid our hands of him.

Lord, Lord! How subject Trump is to his vice of lying.

Trump commits the oldest sins in the newest kind of ways.

Trump's evil acts live in brass: his virtues are written in water.

The evil that men like Trump do lives after them;
The good is often interred with their bones.

A president should bear his country's infirmities,
But Trump makes them greater than they are.

Bell, book, and candle, shall not drive Trump back,
When gold and silver beckons him to come on.

This is the excellent foppery of Trump, that when we are sick in fortune, often the surfeit of his behavior, he makes the sun, the moon, and the stars guilty of his disasters.

He's mad who trusts in the tameness of a wolf or the truth of Trump's promises.

As flies to wanton boys are we to Trumpism - we are killed for its sport.

Wisdom and goodness to Trump seem vile.

Trump is not worth the dust which the rude wind blows in his face.

Trump's but a walking shadow, a poor player,
That struts and frets his hour upon the stage,
And then is heard no more; his is a tale
Told by and idiot, full of sound and fury,
Signifying nothing.

Trump plucks justice by the nose.

Trump is a kind of burr; he shall stick for a long time.

Trump lives to make honesty a vice.

Republicans are dogs, easily won to fawn on Trump.

Every tale condemns Trump for a villain.

For I have sworn Trump fair, and thought him bright,
Who art as black as hell, as dark as night.

How many fond fools serve Trump's madness.

They brought one Trump,
A hungry lean-fac'd villain,
A mere anatomy, a mountebank,
A threadbare juggler, and a fortune-teller,
A need, hollow-ey'd, shard-looking wretch,
A living-dead man.

Trump can cite Scripture for his evil purpose.

We must hold a candle to Trump's shame.

Trump, the man that hath no music in his soul,
Is fit for treasons, stratagems, and spoils.

Though Trump is not naturally honest, he is so sometimes by chance.

Like madness is the glory of Trump's life.

Trump keeps on the windy side of the law.

If the Trump era were play'd upon a stage now,
I could condemn it as an improbable fiction.

Shaw, George Bernard

All that Trump can do for Americans is to shock them and keep them awake at night.

Truth telling is not compatible with Trump's basic nature.

Trump's supposedly a billionaire. That's supposedly his religion.

Trump never does a proper thing without giving an improper reason for it.

When Trump visits overseas, the world locks up its spoons and packs off its womankind.

Trump as King was never born, he was made by artificial hallucination.

Trump thinks he is moral when he is only uncomfortable.

Trump is a celebrity in his circle of hell because lives by robbing the poor.

Physically there is nothing to distinguish the Trump administration from the farm-yard except that Republicans are more troublesome and costly than chickens and its leaders are not so free as cattle.

Trump's golden rule is that there are no golden rules.

Optimistic lies have such therapeutic value for Trump that if he suddenly stopped uttering them he would lose his ability to speak.

Chaos is mother's milk to Trump.

I never expect Trump to think.

Trump's reputation grew with every failure.

Trump prefers a severe preacher because he thinks a few home truths will do his neighbors no harm.

The trouble with Trump is that he is separated from the rest of the country by the same language.

Shaw, Henry Wheeler

Trump is of the firm belief that a good reliable set of bowels is worth more to a man than any quantity of brains.

Shea, Michael

Trump knows that facts are dangerous. They must be controlled and only revealed where essential.

Shelley, Percy Bysshe

Under Trump, the rich have become richer, and the poor have become poorer; and the vessel of the state is driven between the twin monsters of anarchy and despotism.

Sheridan, Phillip Henry

Trump said that if he owned Texas and Hell, he's rent out Texas and live in Hell.

Sheridan, Richard Brinsley

According to Trump, newspapers are the most villainous - licentious - abominable - and infernal ... Not that he ever reads them - No - He makes it a rule to never look into a newspaper.

Trump thinks constant lying is an amiable weakness.

Sherwood, Robert E.

The trouble with Trump is that he is of an increasing race - the anti-intellectuals of America.

Sima Qian

Trumpists, a multitude of evilly disposed people who can stir up strife and are just like a crowd of mosquitos that can make a noise like thunder.

Simic, Charles

Trump is the coyote concert under the window of the room in which the official version of reality is being written.

Simon, Neil

Trump puts on rouge and powder to make his face more attractive. Maybe we can put some make-up on his personality.

There are a million interesting people in our Nation's Capital and precisely zero of them are in the Trump White House.

Sitwell, Edith

Trump may sometimes wish he had time to cultivate modesty... but he is too busy thinking about himself.

Smith, Adam

The chief employment of Trump consists of his constant parade of riches and conspicuous consumption.

Smith, Al

No matter how thin you slice Trump, he's still all baloney.

All the ill's of Trumpism can be cured by more democracy.

Smith, Dodie

Noble deeds are the best cure for Trump.

Smith, Logan

The denunciation of other people is a necessary part of Trump's regimen and greatly assists in his health.

It is the wretchedness of being rich that you have to associate with other rich people … like Trump.

How awful to reflect that what awful things people say about Trump are true.

Trump sold his soul and lives comfortably on the proceeds.

Smith, Roland

Trump will attempt to answer some of your questions intelligently, the more difficult ones will be answered by someone else.

Smith, Sydney

Trump has occasional flashes of silence that make his conversation perfectly delightful.

Trump is prayed for at St. Paul's, but with no very lively hope of success.

Snyder, Gary

Trump could drive a thousand miles without meeting a true friend.

Trump says he couldn't live like some people - this being said by someone who barely knows how to live at all.

Socrates

Trump's false words are not only evil in themselves, but they infect the soul with evil.

Trump should employ his time in improving himself by other men's writings, so that he shall gain easily what others have labored hard for.

You are of courage who does not run away from Trump, but remains at your post and fights against the enemy.

From Trump's deepest desires comes the deadliest hate.

Solon

Laws are like spider webs to Trump; if you are big enough, you can break right through them.

Wrongdoing by Trump can only be cured if those who are not wronged by him feel the same resentment at it as those who are.

Solzhenitsyn, Alexander

The salvation of America lies only in making Trump the concern of all.

For Democrats, Trumpism is a dead dog, while for most Republicans it is a living lion.

Sontag, Susan

In America, the freakish is no longer a private zone. Trump, the Hobbesian man, roams the country, quite visible, with glitter in his hair.

Southey, Robert

Trump's books will be read after Shakespear and Milton are forgotten - and not until then.

Man is easily duped by medical, religious, and political quacks. Trump knows this and acts on it.

Soyinke, Wole

Trump expects to be loved by everyone on the planet.

Trump has an abject lack of courage.

Well, some people say that I'm pessimistic because I recognize that Trump is part of the eternal cycle of evil. All I say is, look at the history of mankind right up to this moment and what do you find?

While President Trump's reign is intolerable, the unknown seems to harbor little risk.

The man dies in all who keep silent in the face of Trumpian tyranny.

Spiel, Hilde

Malace is like a game of poker to Trump; he plays it with all comers.

Spinoza, Baruch

None are more taken in with flattery than proud men like Trump, who wish to be the first and are not.

Stacpoole, Henry

If you have Trump Derangement Syndrome you must keep moving and resisting - it is the only disease that does not require rest.

Stalin, Joseph

Personnel selection is decisive in any organization. People are the most valuable capital. That is why Trump ultimately failed.

Stanley, Edward

The solemn duty of Republicans is to oppose everything and propose nothing.

Steele, Richard

Trump thrives on the insupportable labor of doing nothing.

Stein, Gertrude

There ain't no answer to explain Trump. There ain't going to be any answer. There never has been an answer. That's the answer.

The trouble with Mar-a-Lago is that when you get there, there isn't any there there.

Steinbeck, John

The Republican break with Trump has not come; and the break will never come as long as Trump wields his wrath.

Trump doesn't want advice - he wants corroboration.

Steinem, Gloria

Trump without a woman is like a fish without a bicycle.

Steiner, George

Trump's words that are saturated with lies or atrocity do not easily resume life.

Stephens, James

Men like Trump come of age at about sixty, women at fifteen.

Stern, Richard

A ton of Trump's wit is worth an ounce of other people's. He seems witless.

Sterne, Lawrence

What a happiness it is to Americans, when the anxieties and passions of another day of Trump are over.

Stevens, Anthony

It was Trump's cognitive dissonance that enabled him to go on talking of victory as Joe Biden was knocking on the White House front door. Without this typical wacked characteristic of his, the election may have ended somewhat sooner.

Stevenson, Adlai

My definition of a safe society is a society where it is safe not to believe anything that Trump says.

Trump is the kind of politician who would cut down a redwood tree and then mount the stump for a speech about nature conservation.

When Trump's political ammunition runs low inevitably the rusty artillery of abuse is always wheeled into action.

A lie is an abomination unto the Lord and a very present help to Trump when he's in trouble.

Since the beginning of Trump's administration, his government has been mainly engaged in kicking people around - on both sides.

Trump approaches every question with an open mouth.

Trump is a politician who separates the wheat from the chaff and sells the chaff.

I will make a bargain with Trump. If he stops telling lies about Democrats, we will stop telling the truth about him.

Trump does not live by words alone, although sometimes he has to eat them.

Stevenson, Robert Louis

Trump thinks politics is the only profession for which no preparation is thought necessary.

America should have a grand memory for forgetting Trumpism.

Trump regards common Americans with an indifference bordering on aversion.

Trump sows confusion and reaps indignation.

Stewart, Thomas

Trump can't distinguish between the cost of paying people and investing in them.

Stoll, Clifford

Trump followers are entering a non-existent universe. Consider the consequences.

Stone, Irving

Trump's mind is like a soup dish, wide and shallow; it could hold a small amount of nearly anything.

Donald Trump believed that the least government was the best government; he aspired to become the least President the country ever had and he attained his desire.

Stone, Roger

I launched the idea of Donald J. Trump for President.

Attack, attack, ATTACK — never defend.

Admit nothing, deny everything, launch counterattacks.

Stoppard, Tom

Trump wants to be the center of attention more than to be honest.

The Trump White House is a convention of spiritualists.

Trump is someone who flies around from rally to rally and thinks the most interesting thing about any story is the fact that he has arrived.

Working in Trump's White House is like sharing a cell with a fanatic in search of a mania.

Storr, Anthony

Right-wing conspiracy delusions may be the only thing that makes life tolerable for people who believe in them, and, as such, are jealously defended against all the assaults of reason.

Stout, Rex

For Trump, there are two kinds of statistics, the kind you look up and the kind you make up.

Stravinsky, Igor

Trump is best understood by children and animals.

Too many Trump press conferences finish too long after they end.

Sugar, Alan

Trump's accountants tell him that he has one foot in Jersey, his left earlobe in the Caymans, and his right foot in Zurich, and pays no taxes.

If there was a market for mass-produced portable nuclear weapons, Trump would market them, too.

Suharto

Trump has never been afraid or a party to the multifarious views and opinions expressed by the people.

Sullivan, Anne

It's queer how ready Trump and his people always are with advice in any real or imaginary emergency, and no matter how many times experience has shown them to be wrong, they continue to set forth their opinions, as if they had received them from the Almighy.

Sulpicia

Trump delights in sinning.

Summers, Lawrence H.

Trump always thought that underpopulated countries in Africa were vastly under-polluted.

Trump thinks that the economic logic behind dumping a load of toxic waste in the lowest wage county in America is impeccable.

Swift, Jonathan

Trump conveys a libel in a frown,
And winks a reputation down

I cannot but conclude the bulk of Trump's followers to be the most pernicious race of little vermin that nature ever suffered to crawl upon the surface of the earth.

Trump has spent the four years of his presidency upon a project for extracting sunbeams out of cucumbers, which were to be put into vials hermetically sealed, and let out to warm the air in raw inclement summers.

Trump is so fond of tyrants Vladimir Putin and Kim Jong-un because their political ailment is all the same ... fellow countrymen.

Trump's minions will never quarrel with him, he's their bread and butter.

Trump's promises and pie crusts are meant to be broken.

Trump wears his clothes as though they were thrown on him with a pitchfork.

It is the folly of too many Republicans to mistake a Tweet from the Trump White House for the voice of the country.

Trump is like a man who had a mind to sell Mar-a-Lago, and therefore carries a piece of brick in his pocket, which he shows as a pattern to encourage purchasers.

I never wonder to see a wicked man like Trump, but I often wonder to see them not ashamed.

Swinburne, Algernon

Glory to Trump in the highest! For he is the master of all things.

Szasz, Thomas

Trump is more interested in justifying himself than in better behaving himself.

After Trump, America needs to forgive, but not to forget.

Trump is an illustration of semantic inflation.

T

Taaffe, Eduard

It's Trump's policy to keep everyone in the country in a balanced state of well-modulated distraction, disturbance, and dissatisfaction.

Tacitius

Trump makes a desert and calls it an oasis.

Taft, William Howard

I have come to the conclusion that the major part of the work of President Trump is to increase the receipts of his personal businesses.

Well, Trump has one consolation. No candidate was ever elected ex-president by such a large number of votes.

Talleyrand, Charles

Speech was given to Trump to disguise his thoughts.

Taylor, A. J. P.

If Trump doesn't know enough facts he will still arrive at an answer.

Teale, Edwin

The hardest thing for Trump to do is practice self-restraint.

Tennyson, Alfred

Such as Trump do I remember, who to look upon was to hate.

Teressa of Ávila

Untilled soil, however fertile it may be, will bear thistles and thorns; so it is with Trump's mind.

Tertullian

I believe Trump is a miracle because he is impossible.

Thales

Trumpism is the most ancient of all things, for it had no birth.

There are three attributes for which Trump is grateful to Fortune: that he was born, first, human and not animal; second, man and not woman; and third, American and not barbarian.

Thatcher, Margaret

I always cheer up immensely if an attack from Trump is particularly wounding because I think, well, if he attacks me personally, it means he hasn't a single political argument left.

Theroux, Paul

Trump has made the presidency indistinguishable from rudeness.

Thomas, Dylan

Somebody's boring me, I think it's Trump.

Thomas, Irene

Trump likes the kind of show where the women are not auditioned - they are measured.

Thomas, Norman

Such a little man as Trump should not have made such a big depression.

Thompson, Bonara

Half the misery in the country is caused by ignorance. The other half is caused by Trump.

Thompson, Fred

Trump's still got a lot to learn about Washington. Why, yesterday he accidentally spent some of his own money.

Thompson, Hunter

Trump finally smelling the White House is not much different from a bull elk in the rut. He will stop at nothing, trashing everything that gets in his way.

If Trump were to spill the truth he knows, about six hundred people would be rotting inside prison cells from Moscow to Miami. Absolute truth is a very rare and dangerous commodity in the business of politics, for good reason.

Trump going to trial with lawyers who consider his life-style to be a crime in progress is not a happy prospect.

In a nation ruled by swines like Trump, all pigs are upwardly mobile - and the rest of us are fucked until we can put our acts together: not necessarily to win, but mainly to keep from losing completely.

Thoreau, David

Trump's motto is don't be too moral, you might cheat yourself out of something.

Trump leads a life of unquiet desperation.

Thucydides

What made political war inevitable in modern America has been the growth of the power of Democratic party coalitions and the fear this caused for conservative Republicans.

To Trump all the earth is a tomb.

Tillich, Paul

One of the radicalized and demonical quasi-religions - Trumpism.

Tolson, Melvin

It 's hazardous to shake the Trump family tree. One never knows what will fall out.

Tyrants like Trump don't give a damn about morality.

Tolstoy, Leo

There are no conditions of life to which Trump cannot get accustomed, especially if he sees them accepted by every Republican around him.

Trump sits on the back of America, choking it and making it carry him, and yet Americans assure themselves and others that

Trump must be very sorry for them and wish to ease their lot by all possible means - except by getting off their back.

Trump is like a deaf person who goes on answering questions that no one has asked.

Toole, John Kennedy

You can always tell employees of the Trump White House by the total vacancy which occupies the space where most other people have a face.

Toynbee, Arnold

At bottom, American Trumpism and nationalism are variations of the same perverse theme: Trump's self-centered worship of himself.

Trump does not understand that civilization is a movement, not a condition; it is a voyage, not a harbor.

Tree, Herbert

Trump thinks a committee should consist of himself and two people, both of whom are absent.

Trollope, Anthony

Trump cannot bring himself to believe it possible that any woman should in any respect be wiser than himself. If any such person points out his follies, he at once claims those follies are the special evidence of his genius.

Trotsky, Leon

It was the supreme expression of the mediocrity of the Republican party that Trump rose to its leadership position.

Trump watches his allies just as he watches his enemies.

Truman, Harry S.

Trump is one of the few men in the history of this country to run for high office talking out of both sides of his mouth at the same time and lying out of both sides.

If Trump hadn't been elected President of the United States he probably would have ended up a piano player in a bawdy house.

Herbert Hoover once ran on the slogan "Two cars in every garage." Apparently Trump this year is running on the slogan "Two families in every garage."

Trump is a shifty-eyed goddamn liar … He's one of the few in the history of this country to run for high office talking out of both sides of his mouth and lying out of both sides.

Trump's administration is going to be cussed and discussed for years to come.

If Trump can't convince them, he confuses them.

If Trump wants a friend in Washington, Mar-a-Lago, or anywhere else on the planet, get a dog.

I want that dumb son of a bitch Trump fired.

Tucholsky, Kurt

Trump's ethics can be summed up in two sentences: I ought to. But I won't.

Turgenev, Ivan

Trump has the audacity to believe in nothing.

Tutu, Desmond

We don't want Trumpism liberalized. We want it dismantled. You can't improve something that is intrinsically evil.

Twain, Mark

Human beings are the only animals that blush. Trump never blushes.

Trump is enough to make a body ashamed of the human race.

Trump has no morals, other than that, he seems a fine person.

Trump has never let schooling get in the way of his confusion.

When we recall that Trumpism is mad, the mysteries disappear and life stands explained.

Trump has hardly any more reasoning power of an oyster.

Tynan, Kenneth

Trump is the man who thinks only he knows the way and even then can't drive the car.

U

Udall, Morris

If Trump is elected again, I will run to Mexico and I will fight extradition.

Udall, Stewart L.

Trumpism is like a search and destroy everything mission.

Umalatova, Sazhi

Trump brings in his wake destruction, ruin, blood and tears ... amid the applause of Republicans he has forgotten whose President he is.

Unamuno y Jugo, Miguel de

Trump can conquer many, but he cannot convince.

Republicans see consciousness as a disease.

Updike, John

Trump's governing style is disorganized chaos and madness with a peculiar magnitude.

Trump is proof that the idea of an elder Republican statesman has passed from reality.

That's one of my Goddamn precious American rights, not to think about Trump.

Uris, Leon

Why must we fight for the right to live in Trump's America, over and over, each time the sun rises?

Trump will never understand that the only thing that is going to save America is that if enough people live their lives for something or someone other than themselves.

Ustinov, Peter

Trump is damned to live in the prison of his own mind.

This is a free country, Mr. Trump. We have a right to share your privacy in a public place.

Trump is now a loquacious head-waiter who is allowed to sit down occasionally.

V

Valenzuela, Luisa

God made everything out of nothing. When looking at Trump, the nothingness shows through.

Vallejo, César

Trump was born on a day God was sick.

Vanbrugh, John

Thinking is the greatest fatigue in the world for Trump.

Vanderbilt, William

The public be damned. Trump is working for himself.

Vargas Llosa, Mario

Trumpism is a lack of cultural heritage that pervades all cultures and finds cachet with Republican conservatives, in particular.

The lies of Trump are never gratuitous: they compensate for the inadequacies in his life.

Trump's politics has little to do with ideas, values, and imagination ... and everything to do with maneuvers, intrigues, plots, paranoias, betrayals, a great deal of calculation, no little cynicism, and no lack of con game.

Vauvenargues, Marquis de

Great thoughts come from the heart. Trump has no heart.

We should expect the worst from Trump, as from the weather.

Veblen, Thorstein

Trump's political method reduces itself in the last analyses to the vast use of sabotage.

Véliz, Claudio

Trump thinks he uses speech like a fox, but has the language of a hedgehog.

Vergniaud, Pierre-Victurnien

There is some reason to believe that Trumpism may, like Saturn, devour each of its children one by one.

Verne, Jules

Trump does not joke about such an important matter as his TV ratings. Health of the nation be damned.

Vian, Boris

What concerns Trump is not the happiness of all men, but that of himself.

Victoria

Trump speaks to Me as if I was a public meeting.

Vidal, Gore

For people of a certain age as Trump, litigation takes the place of sex.

Unless drastic reforms occur after Trump's departure, we must accept the fact that every four years the United States will be up for sale, and the richest man or family will buy it.

Whenever a friend succeeds, a little something in Trump dies.

Vigny, Alfred de

Being a good Protestant, Trump loves the majesty of suffering.

Villon, François

Trump seems to know everything but himself.

Virgil

Trump has never, and will never, learn to care for the unfortunate.

From the crime of Trumpism know all Republican leaders as culprits.

The way down to hell for Trump is far too easy a ride.

Vizinczey, Stephen

Trump is a true cosmopolitan. He is unhappy everywhere.

Voinovich, Vladimir

From his close observation of life and his fathoming of life's laws, Trump had understood that it is usually warm in the summer and cold in winter.

That's the storyline of the new GOP - Trump tells lies and Republicans believe them.

A Trump meeting is an arrangement whereby a large number of people gather together, some to say what they really do not think, some not to say what they really do.

Voltaire

Once people begin to reason, Trump knows that all is lost to him.

If Trump does not find anything pleasant, at least he shall find new things to make unpleasant.

Trump uses his thoughts to justify his injustices and his speech to conceal them.

What is Trump's policy? To have erroneous perceptions and to reason entirely from them.

Trump sets the whole world in flames.

Indeed, the Trump era is nothing more than a tableau of crimes and misdemeanors.

Trump is a president who pours laws of which he knows little into a country of which he knows even less.

The fate of America, if not the world, has often depended upon the fragile ego of Trump that day.

Vonnegut, Kurt

Trump believes everybody in America is supposed to grab whatever they can and hang onto it. Some Americans, like himself, are very good at grabbing and holding, and are fabulously well-to-do. Most, though, can't get their hands on diddly-squat.

Trump is full of murderous resentment of people who are as ignorant as he is, without having come by their ignorance the hard way.

Trump thinks the main purpose of the Army, Navy, and Marine Corps is to get poor, stupid Americans into clean, pressed, unpatched clothes, so that rich Americans can stand and gawk at them.

The GOP is a failure. They have written Trumpism on a tablet of salt.

Von Sternberg, Josef

Trump considers that the best way to succeed is to make people hate you.

W

Walker, Margaret

What we have here with Trump is a complete indictment of our present-day society, our whole world. What's wrong with it is money, honey, money.

Wallace, George

If Trump could draw a line in the dust and toss the gauntlet before the feet of America, he would say segregation now, segregation tomorrow, segregation forever!

Wallach, Eli

There's something about a big crowd that brings a lump to Trump's wallet.

Walpole, Horace

It was easier for Trump to conquer the Republican party than know what to do with it.

Walpole, Sir Robert

All those Republicans have their price.

Walton, Isaac

Doubtless God could have made a better Trump, but doubtless he never did.

Ward, Artemus

Trump is happiest when he is idle. He could live for months without performing any kind of labor, and at the expiration of that time he should feel fresh and vigorous enough to go right on in the same way for numerous more months.

Warhol, Andy

Trump is a genius with the IQ of a moron.

Warren, Earl

Republicans consider the things which government does for them to be social progress, but they consider the things government does for others to be socialism.

Warren, Robert Penn

Trumpism is a dime-thin, thumb-worn, two-sided, two-faced con artist coin.

Washington, Booker T.

After the defeat of Trump, there were two points upon which practically all Republican leaders were agreed … that they should change their names, and that they must leave Washington D.C. for at least a few days or weeks in order that they might really feel sure they were free.

Washington, George

From some traits of his character which have lately come to my knowledge, Trump seems to have been so villainous, and so lost to all sense of honor and shame that while his facilities will enable him to continue his sordid pursuits after the presidency, there will be no time for remorse.

Waters, John

In the Trump era people no longer need the jokes explained; everyone gets irony nowadays.

I base everything that Trump does on the idea that he is basically seven years old.

Watts, Alan

Trump's Karma travels with him, like his shadow. Indeed it is his shadow, for Trump stands in his own shadow and wonders why it is dark.

Waugh, Auberon

Trump cannot forgive anything in the way of offense; he cannot forgive any Republican subversion, internal revolution, being contradicted, exposed as a liar, and ridiculed. Additionally, the one thing that he can absolutely never, ever tolerate is being ignored.

I have noticed again and again since I have been in the Church of Republicans that secular interest in GOP matters is often a prelude to delusional thinking.

No Republican leader has been pained by how little pained they've been by Trump's escapades and missteps.

Trump is gifted with the sly, sharp instinct for self-preservation that passes for wisdom among the rich.

Like German opera, Trump is too loud and too long.

Welles, Orson

There are only two emotions within the Trump administration's leadership. Terror and more terror.

In politics, Trump started at the top and worked his way down.

Wellington, Duke of

When a general was asked by Trump what he wanted his speech to be about, the general said "About ten minutes."

Trump's whole life, civil, and political, is a fraud. There is not a transaction, great or small, in which lying and fraud is not introduced.

Wells, H. G.

Trump may be the shape of things to come.

We have come to reliably depend upon Republicans to insert a comfortable time lag of fifty years or a century to intervene between the perception that something ought to be done and the serious attempt to do it.

Wexler, Jerry

Republicans have to capture the lowest common denominator of the voting public. What's wrong with that is that they have to cater to the rancid, infantile, pubescent tastes of Donald Trump.

Wheeler, Charles

Trump has two faults. He doesn't care for politics and he doesn't care for people.

Whistler, James

No one can call Trump a great work of nature.

Trump once said that there were decidedly too many stars and they were not very well arranged. He said he would have done it differently.

Whitehorn, Katherine

Trump's persuasion method includes getting irritated or overbearing in the hope that the dope on the other end of his diatribe will buy whatever it is just to get rid of him.

With creative accounting Trump needs less cheating, but not entirely.

Outside every thin girl is a fat Trump trying to get inside.

Whitton, Charlotte

Whatever women do they must do twice as well as Trump to be thought half as good. Fortunately, that is not difficult.

Wilbur, Richard

The Constitution ... Trump has never read
He had a fine copy, though, which he kept
On a dusty bookcase by his bed
To hang his pants on while he slept.

Wilcox, Ella

Distrust a president like Trump who tells you to distrust.

Wilde, Oscar

Trump knows that a great deal of sincerity is absolutely fatal.

Trump can resist everything except temptation.

Something was dead in Trumpism, and what was dead was Hope.

Really, if the lower orders of people don't set a good example for Trump, what on earth is the use of them?

On an occasion of this kind, meaning the era of Trump, it becomes more than a moral duty to speak one's mind. It becomes a pleasure.

There is only one thing in the world worse for Trump than being talked about, it's not being talked about.

Trump represents the triumph of depravity over morals.

Trump, the man who can dominate a meeting of squirrels, can dominate the GOP.

Trump has Van Gogh's ear for music.

Williams, William Carlos

Trump the Republican,
sniffing at trees,
Just another dog
Among a lot of dogs.

Wilson, Edmund

Of all American Presidents, Trump was probably the most antagonistic towards democracy itself.

Wilson, George F.

Trump, take note: The constitution does not provide for first and second class citizens.

Wilson, Woodrow

Trump is absolutely insincere. That's what makes him so dangerous.

Trump isn't a thorough American if he thinks of America in groups. America does not consist of groups. A president like

Trump who thinks of himself as belonging to a particular national group has not yet become an American.

There are blessed intervals when I forget by one means or another that Trump is President of the United States.

Trump is a man who just sits and thinks, mostly sits.

Wittgenstein, Ludwig

With our attention set on Trump, we are reminded that the human body is not the best picture of the human soul.

Wodehouse, P. G.

If I had to choose between Trump and a cockroach as a companion for a walking tour, the cockroach would have had it by a short head.

What good are brains to Trump? They only unsettle him.

The Trump White House Chief of Staff is a janitor in a loony bin.

Trump is a chubby man who looks as if he has been poured into his suit and forgot to say "When!"

Wolf, Tom

Trump loves to plunge his hands into the dirt.

Woolf, Virginia

The older Trump grows the more he likes indecency.

Trump minds beyond reason the opinions of others.

It is just when Trump's opinions prevail and Republicans have added lip service to their authority that we sometimes become most keenly aware that we do not believe a word we are hearing.

Humor is the first to perish in any Trump endeavor.

Like Mar-a-Lago, we find behind closed communities dotted across America those comfortably padded refuges which are known, euphemistically, as the stately homes of out-of-touch Republicans.

Fate has not been kind to Donald Trump. Nobody listens to him, nobody discusses him, nobody puts him in his place.

Woolcott, Alexander

All the things Trump really likes to do are either immoral, illegal, or fattening.

Mar-a-Lago is just what God would not have done even if he had the money.

Democrats were the cause of Trump just as much as Chicago was responsible for the Chicago Tribune.

There is absolutely nothing wrong with Trump that a miracle cannot fix

Wynne-Tyson, Jon

Trump is the wrong sort of person to be in power because he would not be in power if he was not the wrong sort of person.

Xavier, Saint Francis

Many, many people in the Trump White House are not becoming moralists for one reason only: there is nobody to make them moral.

Tell Trump to give up his small ambitions and come eastward to preach the gospel of the poor.

I want to preach at Trump rallies where there are out and out people worshiping him and only him.

Xenocrates

Trump has never repented speaking, and never of holding his tongue.

Trump's soul is not the source of any genius.

Trump should study the welfare of his country, and not spend his time in feasting and riot.

Xenophanes

Trump always makes gods in his own image.

Trump doesn't know distinctly anything, and he ever will.

If Trump would paint a picture of a god, it would look like himself.

Xerxes

Trump saith: "I am a great king, king of kings, the king of all countries which speak all kinds of languages, the king of the entire big far-reaching earth.

Xu Wenli

In the Trump administration your bag is always packed and behind the door.

Y

Yeats, W. B.

We begin to understand when we have conceived Trumpism as a tragedy.

But was there ever a dog that praised his fleas as Trump does his followers?

Trump has pitched his mansion in the place of excrement.

Yeltsin, Boris

Trump asks forgiveness for not fulfilling some hopes of those people who believed that America would be able to jump from the bright, rich, and civilized past to a grim totalitarian future.

Young, Andrew

Trump proves that political morality is a long way from church morality

Young, Edward

By night Trump half believes in democracy.

Yücel, Can

For Trump, politics is the art of staying out of jail.

Z

Zamyatin, Yevgeny

America cannot continue its progress under the Trump regime, because no creative activity is possible in an atmosphere of systematic persecution that increases in intensity from year to year.

It is hereby proclaimed to all members of the One Trump Republican State: Everyone who is able to do so is obligated to compose treatises, poems, odes, and/or other pieces on the beauty and grandeur of The One Trump Republican State.

Zeno

Trump has two ears and one mouth, so he should listen more than he says.

Zhanguo Ce

Trump, your mansion has plenty of gems and treasures; pools and cars fill up the outbuildings, and there are a lot of beauties in the women's quarters. The only thing your household is short of is righteousness. So I brought you some righteousness.

Zhou Peiyuan

There is a problem in America because under Trump there is a lack of political democracy and academic freedom, which are very important to the development of science.

Zhuangzi

Is not Trump, as compared to all creation, but as the tip of a hair upon a horse's ass?

Trump's judgment passes like a galloping horse, changing at every turn, at every hour. What should he do, what should he not do? He is in a constant state of flux.

Zoshchencko, Mikail

Nobody writes Halloween stories these days, for the good reason that there's nothing particularly hallowed left in our lives under Trump.

Phew! How tough it is to work in the Trump administration. You sweat buckets while trying to hack your way through an impenetrable political jungle of Trump's making. And for what?

The End. Thank God.

EPILOGUE

Quotes by Donald J. Trump

I will be phenomenal to the women. I mean, I want to help women.

Does she (Kim Kardashian) have a good body? No. Does she have a fat ass? Absolutely.

Look at that face (Carly Fiorina). Would anybody vote for that? Can you imagine that, the face of our next president? I mean, she's a woman and I'm not supposed to say bad things, but really, folks, come on.

I refuse to call Megyn Kelly a bimbo, because that would not be politically correct. Instead I will only call her a lightweight reporter!

If I were running The View, I'd fire Rosie O'Donnell. I mean, I'd look at her right in that fat, ugly face of hers, I'd say, 'Rosie, you're fired. Rosie's a person who's very lucky to have her girlfriend and she better be careful or I'll send one of my friends over to pick up her girlfriend. Why would she stay with Rosie if she had another choice? Can you imagine the parents of Kelli ... when she said, 'Mom, Dad, I just fell in love with a big, fat pig named Rosie?'

(Stormy Daniels is a) Horseface.

I know where she (Hillary Clinton) went, it's disgusting, I don't want to talk about it ... No, it's too disgusting. Don't say it, it's disgusting.

(Hillary Clinton is) such a nasty woman.

(Senator Kamala Harris) was very, very nasty, to — one of the reasons that surprised me, she was very — she was probably nastier than even Pocahontas (Senator Elizabeth Warren) to Joe Biden.

This monster (Senator Kamala Harris) was onstage with Mike Pence.

I looked forward to going but I thought the prime minister's (female Danish Prime Minister Mette Frederiksen) statement that it was 'absurd,' that it was an absurd idea, was nasty.

I think [Pelosi is] a disgrace. I actually don't think she's a talented person. I've tried to be nice to her because I would have liked to have gotten some deals done. She's incapable of doing deals. She's a nasty, vindictive, horrible person.

I'm allowed to go in because I'm the owner of the pageant and therefore I'm inspecting it... You know, they're standing there with no clothes. And you see these incredible looking young women and so, I sort of get away with things like that.

I didn't know that she (Duchess of Sussex, Meghan Markle) was nasty.

What is it when a woman is 35 years old? It's called check-out time.

(Omarosa Manigault-Newman is) a crazed, crying lowlife and a dog. When you give a crazed, crying lowlife a break and give her a job at the White House, I guess it just didn't work out. Good work by General Kelly for quickly firing that dog!

(Arianna Huffington is) unattractive both inside and out. I fully understand why her former husband left her for a man — he made a good decision.

What do you think of Lindsay Lohan? There's something there, right? But you have to like freckles. I've seen a close-up of her chest.

And a lot of freckles. Are you into freckles? ... She's probably deeply troubled and therefore great in bed. How come the deeply troubled women — deeply, deeply troubled — they're always the best in bed?

(Ivanka Trump) does have a very nice figure ... if (she) weren't my daughter, perhaps I'd be dating her.

Bette Midler talks about my hair but I'm not allowed to talk about her ugly face or body --- so I won't.

You know, it doesn't really matter what (the media) writes as long as you've got a young and beautiful piece of ass.

I've got to use some Tic Tacs, just in case I start kissing her. You know I'm automatically attracted to beautiful — I just start kissing them. It's like a magnet. Just kiss. I don't even wait. And when you're a star, they let you do it. You can do anything ... Grab them by the pussy. You can do anything.

Oftentimes when I was sleeping with one of the top women in the world I would say to myself, thinking about me as a boy from Queens, 'Can you believe what I am getting?'

I moved on her actually. You know she was down on Palm Beach. I moved on her and I failed. I'll admit it. I did try and fuck her. She was married.

You could see there was blood coming out of her (Megan Kelly's) eyes. Blood coming out of her wherever.

All of the women on The Apprentice flirted with me - consciously or unconsciously. That's to be expected.

The only card she has is the woman's card. She's got nothing else to offer and frankly, if Hillary Clinton were a man, I don't think she'd get 5 percent of the vote. The only thing she's got going is the woman's card and the beautiful thing is, women don't like her.

(When asked if he would stay with [his wife] if she was disfigured in a car crash:) "How do the breasts look?"

You've got to deny, deny, deny and push back on these women. If you admit to anything and any culpability, then you're dead. ... You've got to be strong. You've got to be aggressive. You've got to push back hard. You've got to deny anything that's said about you. Never admit.

Who wouldn't take Kate's (Middleton, Duchess of Cambridge) picture and make lots of money if she does the nude sunbathing thing. Come on Kate!

(On Angelina Jolie:) "I remember at the Academy Awards a few years ago she was frenching her brother. She was giving her brother lip kisses like I never saw before in my life. And she had just said she made love to Billy Bob Thornton in the back of the limousine on the way over. And I wouldn't want to shake her hand, by the way.

I heard poorly rated Morning Joe speaks badly of me (don't watch anymore). Then how come low I.Q. Crazy Mika, along with Psycho Joe, came to Mar-a-Lago 3 nights in a row around New Year's Eve and insisted on joining me. She was bleeding badly from a face-lift. I said no!

While Bette Midler is an extremely unattractive woman, I refuse to say that because I always insist on being politically correct.

I would never buy Ivana any decent jewels or pictures. Why give her negotiable assets?

My favourite part (of Pulp Fiction) is when Sam has his gun out in the diner and he tells the guy to tell his girlfriend to shut up. 'Tell that bitch to be cool. Say: Bitch be cool.' I love those lines.

Certain guys tell me they want women of substance, not beautiful models. It just means they can't get beautiful models.

Nobody has more respect for women than I do. Nobody. Nobody has more respect.

My fingers are long and beautiful, as it has been well documented, are various other parts of my body.

Why would Kim Jong-un insult me by calling me "old," when I would NEVER call him "short and fat?" Oh well, I try so hard to be his friend - and maybe someday that will happen!

Mike Pompeo is doing a great job, I am very proud of him. His predecessor, Rex Tillerson, didn't have the mental capacity needed. He was dumb as a rock and I couldn't get rid of him fast enough. He was lazy as hell.

Every time I speak of the haters and losers I do so with great love and affection. They cannot help the fact that they were born fucked up!

....Actually, throughout my life, my two greatest assets have been mental stability and being, like, really smart. Crooked Hillary Clinton also played these cards very hard and, as everyone knows, went down in flames. I went from VERY successful businessman, to top T.V. star to President of the United States (on my first try). I think that would qualify as not smart, but genius....and a very stable genius at that!

The FAKE NEWS media (failing @nytimes, @NBCNews, @ABC, @CBS, @CNN) is not my enemy, it is the enemy of the American People!

If the morons who killed all of those people at Charlie Hebdo (Paris, France) would have just waited, the magazine would have folded - no money, no success!

I strongly pressed President Putin twice about Russian meddling in our election. He vehemently denied it.

An 'extremely credible source' has called my office and told me that Barack Obama's birth certificate is a fraud.

I would like to extend my best wishes to all, even the haters and losers, on this special date, September 11th.

Why should I go to that (military) cemetery? It's filled with losers. I don't get it. What was in it for them?

Who were the good guys in this war (World War I)?

He's (Senator John McCain) not a war hero, I like people who weren't captured.

It's really cold outside, they are calling it a major freeze, weeks ahead of normal. Man, we could use a big fat dose of global warming!

The concept of global warming was created by and for the Chinese in order to make U.S. manufacturing non-competitive.

I'm the most successful person ever to run for the presidency, by far. Nobody's ever been more successful than me. I'm the most successful person ever to run.

I look very much forward to showing my financials, because they are huge.

The concept of shaking hands is absolutely terrible and statistically I've been proven right.

I think Viagra is wonderful if you need it, if you have medical issues, if you've had surgery. I've just never needed it. Frankly, I wouldn't mind if there were an anti-Viagra, something with the opposite effect. I'm not bragging. I'm just lucky. I don't need it.

I could stand in the middle of 5ᵗʰ Avenue and shoot somebody and I wouldn't lose voters.

Why are we having all these people from shithole countries coming here?

I would bet if you took a poll in the FBI I would win that poll by more than anybody's won a poll.

(Kim Jong-Un) speaks and his people sit up at attention. I want my people to do the same.

Nobody has better respect for intelligence than Donald Trump.

North Korean Leader Kim Jong-Un just stated that the "Nuclear Button is on his desk at all times." Will someone from his depleted and food starved regime please inform him that I too have a Nuclear Button, but it is a much bigger & more powerful one than his and my Button works!

I'm the least racist person you have ever interviewed.

I guess you would start off by saying, 'England.' Right? You know, I ask Boris (Johnson), 'Where's England? What's happening with England?' They don't use it too much anymore.

What you're seeing and what you're reading is not what's happening.

Nobody knew health care could be so complicated.

I loved my previous life. I had so many things going. This is more work than in my previous life. I thought it (U.S. Presidency) would be easier.

I had a meeting at the Pentagon with lots of generals -- they were like from a movie, better looking than Tom Cruise and stronger -- and I had more generals than I've ever seen.

The buck stops with everybody.

There are those that think I am a very stable genius, OK?

Under the normal rules, I'll be out in 2024 so we may have to go for an extra term.

We can expect that, by spring (2020), we will be well on our way to recovery (from the COVID-19 pandemic). We think, by June 1, a lot of great things will be happening.

We can have a lot of fun tonight. I have nothing to do. Nothing. Nothing.

Democrats can't find a Smocking gun tying the Trump campaign to Russia after James Comey's Testimony. No Smocking gun.

I take advantage of the laws of the nation. Because I'm running a company.

Are you allowed to impeach a president for gross incompetence?

Sorry losers and haters, but my I.Q. is one of the highest -and you all know it! Please don't feel so stupid or insecure, it's not your fault.

Happy Cinco De Mayo! The best taco bowls are made in Trump Tower Grill. I love Hispanics!

How amazing, the State Health Director who verified copies of Obama's "birth certificate" died in plane crash today. All others lived.

If you don't support me, you're going to be so goddamn poor.

You know, you had governors and senators, you know they were all good until I beat the shit out of them, O.K.?

We have (COVID-19) totally under control. It's one person coming in from China. It's going to be just fine. (January, 2020)

Looks like by April (2020), you know in theory when it gets a little warmer, (COVID-19) miraculously goes away. (February, 2020)

I think that's a problem that's going to go away... They have studied (COVID-19). They know very much. In fact, we're very close to a vaccine. (February, 2020)

The 15 (COVID-19 cases in the US) within a couple of days is going to be down to close to zero. (February, 2020)

This is a flu (COVID-19). This is like a flu. (February, 2020)

(COVID-19 is) going to disappear. One day, it's like a miracle, it will disappear. (February, 2020)

I like this stuff. I really get it. People are surprised that I understand (COVID-19)... Every one of these doctors said, 'How do you know so much about this?' Maybe I have a natural ability. Maybe I should have done that instead of running for president. (March, 2020)

No, I'm not concerned at all (about COVID-19). (March, 2020)

I don't take responsibility at all (re: Trump's administration's COVID-19 response). (March, 2020)

The only thing we haven't done well is get good press. (March, 2020)

I intended "to always play (COVID-19) down." (March, 2020)

I say that you're a terrible reporter, that's what I say. I think it's a very nasty question, and I think it's a very bad signal that you're putting out to the American people." [Response to reporter's question: "What do you say to Americans who are watching you right now who are scared?"] (March, 2020)

We've never closed down the country for the flu," Trump said. "So you say to yourself, what is this (COVID-19 pandemic) all about? (March, 2020)

They (governors of individual states) have to treat us well, also. They can't say, 'Oh, gee, we should get this, we should get that.' (March, 2020)

I couldn't have done it any better. [When asked if his coronavirus response could have been better] (April, 2020)

[w]hen somebody's the president of the United States, the authority is total. (April, 2020)

Look, we're going to lose anywhere from 75,000, 80,000 to 100,000 people (May, 2020)

This (COVID-19) is going to go away without a vaccine. It is going to go away. We are not going to see it again. (May, 2020)

Could be that (COVID-19) testing's, frankly, overrated. Maybe it is overrated. (May, 2020)

We've done a GREAT job on Covid response, making all Governors look good, some fantastic (and that's OK), but the Lamestream Media doesn't want to go with that narrative, and the Do Nothing Dems talking point is to say only bad about "Trump". I made everybody look good, but me! (May, 2020)

It's (COVID-19) going away. (June, 2020)

They (Americans) are dying. That's true. And you — it is what it is. (August, 2020)

I don't wear a mask like him (presidential candidate Joe Biden). Every time you see him, he's got a mask. He could be speaking 200 feet away from him and he shows up with the biggest mask I've ever seen. (September, 2020)

People are saying whatever. Just leave us alone. They're tired of (COVID-19). People are tired of hearing (infectious disease expert) Fauci and all these idiots...Fauci is a nice guy. He's been here for 500 years. (October, 2020)

They are getting tired of the pandemic, aren't they? You turn on CNN, that's all they cover. 'Covid, Covid, Pandemic, Covid, Covid.' You know why? They're trying to talk everybody out of voting. People aren't buying it, CNN, you dumb bastards. (October, 2020)

Covid, Covid, Covid is the unified chant of the Fake News Lamestream Media. They will talk about nothing else until November 4th., when the Election will be (hopefully!) over. Then the talk will be how low the death rate is, plenty of hospital rooms, & many tests of young people. (October, 2020)

Our doctors get more money if someone dies from Covid, and so 'when in doubt' choose Covid. (October, 2020)

[Author's note: In December, 2020, American deaths exceeded 300,000, more than all U.S. combat deaths in all theaters of WW II]

...the only way we're going to lose this (2020) election is if the election is rigged. Remember that. It's the only way we're going to lose this election...

Lightning Source UK Ltd.
Milton Keynes UK
UKHW010350281220
375877UK00011B/838/J